IDEAS OF ORDER

Ideas of Order

A CLOSE READING OF
SHAKESPEARE'S SONNETS

Neil L. Rudenstine

FARRAR, STRAUS AND GIROUX

NEW YORK

Farrar, Straus and Giroux
18 West 18th Street, New York 10011

Copyright © 2014 by Neil L. Rudenstine
Printed in the United States of America
Published in 2014 by Farrar, Straus and Giroux
First paperback edition, 2015

The Library of Congress has cataloged the hardcover edition as follows:
Rudenstine, Neil L.
    Ideas of order : a close reading of Shakespeare's sonnets / Neil L. Rudenstine. —
First edition.
        pages   cm
    Includes bibliographical references (p.   ).
    ISBN 978-0-374-28015-4 (hardback) — ISBN 978-0-374-71201-3 (e-book)
    1. Shakespeare, William, 1564–1616. Sonnets.   I. Title.

PR2848 .R83 2014
821'.3—dc23

                                                                    2014014642

Paperback ISBN: 978-0-374-53573-5

Designed by Jonathan D. Lippincott

Our books may be purchased in bulk for promotional, educational,
or business use. Please contact your local bookseller or the
Macmillan Corporate and Premium Sales Department at
1-800-221-7945, extension 5442, or by e-mail at
MacmillanSpecialMarkets@macmillan.com.

www.fsgbooks.com
www.twitter.com/fsgbooks • www.facebook.com/fsgbooks

P1

For Antonia, Nicholas, and Sonya

Contents

A Note on the Text

During the course of writing this volume, I have consulted several editions of the Sonnets, using the 1609 version as a constant reference point. Colin Burrow's excellent edition (New York: Oxford, 2002) has been especially helpful, but no single version has been followed. When faced with important differences among authorities, I have made my own choices.

IDEAS OF ORDER

ONE

Inner Order

Shakespeare's Sonnets are the greatest single work of lyric poetry in English, and many of the individual poems are as powerful as those in any language. Yet they are scarcely read, except for the few that are regularly anthologized. This is not necessarily surprising. The vogue for sonnets reached its height in England during the last decades of the sixteenth century, and while many major writers—including Milton, Wordsworth, Keats, Frost, and Auden—have at times used the form to great effect, it remains a rarity, especially in modern literature.

To be confronted with a sequence of 154 sonnets, therefore, is a considerable challenge, particularly if the poems are as complex as any work written by Shakespeare. To try to take the measure of each of these poems is an exercise for adventurous but also patient spirits. To grasp the contours of the sequence as a whole requires no less concentration. The effort, however, is more than simply rewarding, because the work consists of love poetry that is as passionate, daring, intimate, searing, and lyrical as any that we may ever encounter.

This book is intended as an introduction for readers who may have an interest in the Sonnets themselves, or in Shakespeare's work as a whole, or simply in lyric poetry. It makes no attempt to survey the broad range of comparatively recent interpretations, but does argue that the Sonnets are more carefully ordered—as a coherent sequence—than is the case in most other works of criticism and scholarship.

•

A number of the best Shakespearean scholars have—over a great many years—shown how little evidence exists to support any number of hypotheses put forward by commentators with an interest in the historical or biographical background of the Sonnets. But these efforts were, for a very long time, largely ignored. The situation was such that in 1964 when W. H. Auden published an introduction to the sequence, he began not with the usual generalizations that characterize such essays, but with a full assault:

> Probably, more nonsense has been talked and written, more intellectual and emotional energy expended in vain, on the sonnets of Shakespeare than on any other literary work in the world . . . It so happens that we know almost nothing about the historical circumstances under which Shakespeare wrote these sonnets: we don't know to whom they are addressed or exactly when they were written, and unless entirely new evidence should turn up, which is unlikely, we never shall.

Auden's piece was a swashbuckling venture in which he tried to scatter the tribes of all those who have searched, without persuasive results, for the person who is enigmatically called the "Onlie Begetter" of the poems, and whose initials (on the title page of the 1609 original edition) are "Mr. W. H." Auden also tried to sweep away speculation about the origin of the various "characters" in the Sonnets, including the young man (with whom the poet is in love); the so-called dark lady (the poet's mistress and object of his lust); and the "rival poet" with his "compeers by night." There is not, as Auden and others have rightly pointed out, a reliable piece of evidence to confirm the identity of any of these figures.

Finally, Auden tried to detonate any lingering belief that the Sonnets were autobiographical in nature, although he did—rather oddly—view them as a kind of diary written by the poet "for himself alone." In Auden's view, Shakespeare played no part in preparing the poems for publication: they were simply too intimate, and "Shakespeare must have been horrified" when they suddenly appeared in print.

Apart from biographical and more general historical matters, at least two other major issues have confronted commentators. These concern the order of the Sonnets and their dating. Although contemporary scholars and critics differ about the extent and nature of the Sonnets' order, many would agree that there are a number of tightly linked "clusters" of poems that focus on either a particular situation, or incident, or theme—and these clusters are clearly relevant to any intelligent reading of the entire work. Indeed, some editors, over many decades, have attempted to rearrange the sequence in an effort to create a more fully coherent and carefully structured narrative or drama. Not surprisingly, all of these attempts failed.

Sonnet sequences belong to no well-defined genre. If one compares the sonnets of Petrarch, Sidney, Spenser, Daniel, and Drayton, one grasps immediately how much latitude was offered to the poet who set out to write yet another "collection." Moreover, because some (not all) of these works were written over a period of years, there was ample time for digressions, turnings, and returnings to themes and preoccupations that could be initially explored in a few sonnets, temporarily set aside, and then taken up again at a later point. In addition, inexplicable (as well as explicable) gaps—or poems that seem to be entirely "misplaced"—can suddenly appear. As a result, the reader or critic may well conclude (as did Auden) that there is finally no clear order to Shakespeare's sequence.

By contrast, Richard Blackmur's essay on the Sonnets, published in 1961, offered a view that is helpful in a number of respects:

No one can improve upon the accidentally established order we possess; but everyone can invite himself to feel the constant interflow of new relations, of new reticulations—as if the inner order were always on the move . . . Furthermore . . . the sequence we have seems sensible with respect to [the poems'] sentiments, and almost a "desirable" sequence with respect to the notion of development.

For Blackmur, the unfolding pattern of the Sonnets' "sentiments" and the arc of the work's "development" seemed right. He believed that the order of the poems reflected Shakespeare's intentions, and he proposed that those who disagreed should try reading the poems in reverse order: "They will turn themselves round again of their own force." Although Shakespeare's role in arranging the poems remains open to speculation, some of the clusters of linked sonnets seem so tightly bound together that it is hard to imagine he played no substantive part in their formation.

If Shakespeare was concerned about giving some discernible shape to the Sonnets, there is no way to settle the question of his role in their publication. Perhaps his informal audience of friends was sufficient. Circulating one's poems privately was of course not unusual during the Elizabethan period: Sidney certainly showed no interest in publishing his own sonnet sequence, *Astrophil and Stella*, and Donne would almost certainly have been embarrassed to see his *Songs and Sonnets* in print. With respect to Shakespeare, there is simply no way to reach a persuasive conclusion: the case remains open, and is likely to remain so.

•

Most scholars are inclined to date the Sonnets—at least in large part—to the early to mid-1590s, which is plausible on stylistic grounds. Moreover, Shakespeare made use of the sonnet form in some of his plays from the same period (such as *Love's Labor's Lost* and *Romeo and Juliet*), while he also explored situations in the

Sonnets that resemble scenes from *Two Gentlemen of Verona* and *A Midsummer Night's Dream*. We know that a number of the sonnets had been written and were in circulation by 1598. Francis Meres, in a "review" of then-current literature, referred specifically to Shakespeare's "sugred sonnets among his private friends"; and two of the sonnets (138 and 144) appeared in a 1599 anthology.

Although many of the poems were composed at a relatively early stage in Shakespeare's career, it is hard to imagine that a number of them (especially after sonnets 107–108) were written much before the late 1590s, perhaps the early 1600s. Several of these later sonnets to the young man deal at a consistently deep level with the themes of infatuation, betrayal, self-betrayal, disillusion, and moments of attempted reconciliation and affirmation. Similar themes appear early in the sequence, but many poems (beginning with 109) reveal a density and relentlessness of torturous experience—with some obvious moments of asserted triumph but no final resolution.

There are many ways to approach the Sonnets, and several excellent scholarly books (and editions) in recent decades have highlighted one or another method. It is possible, for example, to analyze Shakespeare's Sonnets in the light of other sequences, reaching back to Petrarch; or to relate major themes in the Sonnets to those in selected Shakespeare plays; or to think of each sonnet as an individual lyric, with a formal structure of its own; or to emphasize the misogynistic aspects—or the homoerotic aspects—of the work.

It is rare to find consideration of the sequence as if it had some of the characteristics of a drama or narrative, and there are certainly reasons not to do so. The Sonnets have no fully substantial "characters" except for the poet: the others are accessible only through his eyes, so we must infer the feelings, motives, actions, and attitudes of the young man or the so-called dark lady from what the poet says. As a result, a great deal of what happens remains obscure. When the young man first betrays and deserts the poet (in sonnets 33–35), we learn only the most general nature of his transgression. If we try to trace an overarching line of development, we risk being drawn into something close to Auden's conception of the Sonnets as a kind of diary, written by the poet for "himself alone." And we may be tempted (for the sake of the work's continuity) to discover connections where there are none, or to find coherence when there may be only disorder. Consequently, many of the best Shakespearean scholars and critics have (in the past three to four decades) concluded that it is impossible to discover any substantial degree of unity in the Sonnets. Several have suggested that some of the sonnets attributed to the friend may have been written with a woman in mind, because many of the poems lack "gendered" pronouns. Still others find too many discontinuities—from poem to poem—to allow for much or any coherence at all in the work.

These are all relevant observations, and anyone who wishes to make the case for a particular kind of order in the sequence must assume (as this book does) that there is one male friend in the first 126 sonnets, and one mistress in 127–54; that some sections are concerned with identifiable themes, in contrast to quite well-defined specific incidents and situations; and that one can trace an overall progression of sentiments and a general development in the work, even though many individual poems do not strictly follow the subject matter of those immediately preceding them.

In considering this apparent lack of continuity, several points should be kept in mind. First, the love between the poet and the friend is sufficiently mutual—although not equal in intensity—that it survives any number of serious lapses or transgressions. Indeed, it continues to the very end of the first 125 sonnets, and is clearly alluded to in the final section of the sequence. This love is utterly transformative for the poet, and he remains firmly devoted to it, regardless of the friend's (as well as his own) unfaithfulness. Love binds the poet in an irresistible way, and he is willing to suffer any number of humiliations and temporary repudiations without seriously risking a full break in the relationship with the young man.

Although the relationship is defined primarily in terms of love, the poet becomes, very early in the sequence, the friend's chosen or favored writer, and this means he is initially drawn to create poems of praise intended to celebrate, engage, impress, and at times amuse the friend. Consequently, unless the poet is willing to renounce the relationship (which he is not), he must chart a course that will eventually include sonnets of suspicion, dismay, and accusation in the light of the friend's successive betrayals, as well as sonnets that are committed to a mode of compliment, praising the young man's beauty, "worth," and even constancy.

As a result, many of the poet's unexpected changes in stance, tone, and subject matter derive from his need to maintain these conflicting roles. He is at moments a critic and accuser of the young man, while he must also—if he is to remain "favored"—continue to satisfy the youth's desire for poetry, which is often difficult to distinguish from mere flattery. Given this situation, we should expect to find many instances of the poet shifting from recrimination— even verbal "attack"—to praise and even self-denigration, sometimes stressing the former quite fiercely, but soon reverting to the latter. Such a pattern emerges in the movement from sonnets 33–35 on the one hand, to 36–39 on the other; then again 67–70 followed by 71–74; and again 87 followed by 88–90.

Perhaps the most conspicuous of these examples occurs after the rival poet series (76–86) when the poet, having been rejected by the friend, bids "Farewell" (87) to the young man, ultimately accusing him of being a "mansion" of "vices" and a "base" jewel (95–96). This assault comes closer to causing a total break in the relationship than any previous incident, but it is followed by sonnet 97, which—in a completely different vein—is clearly a poem of strongly expressed love. We may well feel that we are faced with a radical "disconnect" that is inexplicable. But 97 starts with the line "How like a winter hath my absence been / From thee," and sonnet 98 opens in a similar way ("From you have I been absent"). These and other poems in this group make clear that a period of estrangement followed the poet's attack on the friend in sonnets 94–96, and this prolonged absence has finally led to a full reunion. Indeed, sonnets 97–108 include some of the most beautiful and marvelously lyrical in the entire sequence, and they celebrate a renewal of mutual deep affection when the poet praises not simply the friend's beauty, but his recommitment to the love relationship.

A note on the issue of patronage: throughout this volume, I refer to the poet as the friend's *chosen* or *favored* writer—terms that suggest a conventional patronage relationship. And the poet refers often enough to the young man as if he were indeed a patron of considerable status who would in some way reward him, if not financially, at least with the honor of having a "superior" person "accept" his work.

The Sonnets, however, present us with an exceptionally complex case. Important elements of patronage exist, but the poet's frequent critique of the friend, and the intimate nature of the love, take us well beyond anything conventional. The dedications to patrons by other Elizabethan writers (such as Spenser) are highly formal and characterized by unqualified praise. Nothing remotely approaching criticism appears, and there is certainly no presumption that there might be a close relationship between patron and writer.

The Sonnets exist, therefore, in their own realm: they often present the friend as a "lord" or a "sun" looking down on the poet's netherworld; by contrast, they sometimes define the friend as a near-equal in mutual love—or else as someone who is unfaithful, unfathomable, and even (as suggested) a "mansion" of "vices." As a result, I have avoided the terms *patron* and *patronage*, but have used *chosen* or *favored* writer to characterize the poet: this approach sacrifices a measure of precision, but it has the advantage of being descriptive without imposing a traditional (and more strictly defined) conception on the sequence.

TWO

Desirable Development

If this volume traces the line of "almost desirable" development suggested by Richard Blackmur, there are several arguments in favor of such an approach. Even the least "dramatic" reading of the Sonnets makes it impossible to avoid talking about "the young man," or the rival poet, or the dark lady. One cannot treat the so-called marriage poems, or the friend's successive infidelities, or the rival poet series, or the poet's betrayal of the friend, without discussing the unfolding of these incidents, including the ways in which the poet (and others) appear to act (and react) to them. Moreover, the reader is inevitably involved—as an observer and interpreter—in these situations, and has no escape from this role.

An approach of this kind is possible only because there is, in my view, sufficient scaffolding to support it. There are a number of clusters of poems related to particular characters and events, as well as themes. They include:

> *Sonnets 1–20*: The "marriage poems" and their immediate aftermath, when an apparent mutual love between the poet and the friend is acknowledged.
> *Sonnets 21–32*: Poems of praise in which the poet also reveals his misgivings about the friend's faithfulness.
> *Sonnets 33–36*: Following these doubts, the friend in fact betrays and abandons the poet. He then returns contrite:

he weeps, and there is an obvious reunion between the two men. In pardoning the young man, however, the poet declares that he has "corrupted" himself by excusing the transgression.

Sonnets 37–39: Poems of longing and of praise when the two men are separated.

Sonnets 40–42: The friend and the poet's mistress are jointly unfaithful to the poet. The poet is now more assertive than before (33–35) in his condemnation of the young man (and the mistress).

Sonnets 43–75: The poet ventures to discover and define the nature of the friend's character. In the course of this quest, he comes closer to an explicit "assault" on the young man (69–70). Then suddenly he expresses serious doubts about his own "worth" and that of his poetry (71–72), before ending on a positive note (74).

Sonnets 76–86: The friend entertains the possibility of choosing another favored writer. He ends with a (temporary) rejection of the poet and his "style" in favor of a rival.

Sonnets 87–96: In the wake of this rejection, the poet bids the friend "Farewell" (87) but does not give up hope of sustaining the relationship. He envisions the possibility of being entirely repudiated (88–90) by the young man. Then, soon after, he embarks on a full attack—the most aggressive in the sequence—on the friend's character (94–96).

Sonnets 97–108: A lengthy separation follows sonnet 96; sonnet 97 signals a return of the poet to the friend and a clear reconciliation.

Sonnets 109–20: The poet is himself unfaithful to the friend, but the two men are eventually reunited.

Sonnets 121–26: Poems of self-affirmation by the poet, with renewed professions of love, which is now defined in a new way—prefigured by sonnets 116 and 119–20.

Sonnets 127–54: Poems to the mistress, with increasing indications of the poet's deep self-betrayal and lack of control in the face of lust. Three poems (133, 134, 144) allude
to the friend's similar subjugation.

From this outline, we can begin to trace one significant—
indeed central—way in which the sequence develops. Among
several themes, it explores a continuing series of betrayals or transgressions by the two main figures, from the beginning to the end
of the work. In this sense, the usual division between the first 126
poems to the young man, and the remainder to the mistress, is not
altered, but is less emphatic than it may at first seem. Instead, there
is considerable continuity and, as a result, we can see how the poet
and the friend undergo constant—and similar—transformations
throughout the course of the entire 154 sonnets.

Early in the sequence, after the poet is first betrayed by the
friend, he proceeds to "corrupt" himself by pardoning and excusing the young man's infidelity. After another "offence" by the youth,
the poet becomes even more abject, offering to defend and even
praise the young man in spite of all that has happened. Later, the
poet is himself unfaithful to the friend, and finally he succumbs
entirely to the mistress, becoming a slave to "lust in action." By the
end of the sequence, he has disintegrated in the face of uncontrollable desire.

Meanwhile, the friend undergoes an analogous progression.
Following an initial profession of love to the poet, he is persis-
tently unfaithful. Then his deliberate repudiation of the poet in
favor of a rival strikes home with even greater force than his earlier
transgressions. Finally, the friend (like the poet) becomes helpless
in the face of the dark lady. The poet asks her, "Is't not enough to
torture me alone, / But slave to slavery my sweet'st friend must
be?" (133). The friend has completely capitulated: he is now a passive instrument—a "slave"—to the mistress.

In short, the two sections of the sequence—combined, as a

single work—track the continuous "fall" of both the poet and the friend. Each of the two major figures moves from the early prospect of potential mutual love to episodes of unfaithfulness and betrayal, to complete helplessness in the face of lust—so much so that the poet ultimately acknowledges, "I do betray / My nobler part to my gross body's treason" (151).

Another major line of development involves an effort by the poet to probe the character of the friend, with each concentrated probe resulting in a deeper and more daring indictment of the young man. After the youth's first desertion (in sonnet 33), the poet responds with a number of controlled complaints (including a good deal of self-pity), which lead to the friend's hastened return (34). The two men are reunited, and the young man even weeps in contrition (34). Following the friend's next offense, however, the poet responds more forcefully with open bitterness, including a great deal of accusatory mock-wit (40–42). He ventures to describe the youth as "Lascivious grace, in whom all ill well shows." Nevertheless, he moves quickly to "excuse" the friend, declaring himself willing to accept whatever is dealt him: "Kill me with spites; yet we must not be foes."

The next set of sonnets (43–70) marks an increasing effort to define the nature of the young man. But by this point, the youth—in a further turn of events—has claimed the full freedom to go where (and with whom) he pleases. The poet is left with no choice: unwilling to break off the relationship, he accepts the friend's new license and is soon reduced to a state of (often abject) powerlessness, waiting upon the young man's beck and call. In time, however, his verse becomes more assertive (68–69). Slanderous "churls" have said the youth is so promiscuous that he has the "rank smell of weeds" (69) and the poet implicitly agrees, adding (in the couplet) that the young man's "odour" fails to match his appearance because he has grown "common."

This development ultimately ends in sonnets 87–96, following the trauma of the (temporary) rejection of the poet in favor of a rival—the most lacerating of his infidelities—prompting the poet to become far more audacious and accusatory than at any previous time. He refers to the friend (in 95) as a "mansion" of "vices," and exclaims, "O, in what sweets dost thou thy sins enclose!" Such a climactic "discovery" and unmasking of the young man brings this line of the action to a finale (although the poet's assault turns out to be only a prelude to further unanticipated events that will soon follow).

THREE

Eternal Lines

If the Sonnets lend themselves to being read as a sequence, with a discernible but not always strict order, most of the individual poems ought to gain in meaning and implication depending on their placement. Sonnet 18, "Shall I compare thee to a summer's day," is a particularly striking example of a familiar poem that is often anthologized as a single "independent" lyric, yet its meaning is significantly transformed simply by moving it from a "school text" to its rightful position in the sequence:

> Shall I compare thee to a summer's day?
> Thou art more lovely and more temperate:
> Rough winds do shake the darling buds of May,
> And summer's lease hath all too short a date;
> Sometime too hot the eye of heaven shines,
> And often is his gold complexion dimmed;
> And every fair from fair sometime declines,
> By chance, or nature's changing course untrimmed:
> But thy eternal summer shall not fade,
> Nor lose possession of that fair thou ow'st,
> Nor shall Death brag thou wand'rest in his shade,
> When in eternal lines to time thou grow'st.
> > So long as men can breathe or eyes can see,
> > So long lives this, and this gives life to thee.
> >   (18)

When read as a single poem on its own, the meaning of sonnet 18 seems clear. The poet praises the summerlike beauty of another person, and insists that neither the person nor the beauty will ever die: they will be forever immortalized in his verse. If we were to read dozens of Elizabethan (and earlier) poems, we would find countless examples in which a poet celebrates the physical—and often spiritual—qualities of his lady. The immortality theme is also familiar, reaching back to classical verse. And the constant enmity of Time is no less common. Finally, the poet's assertion of his own power, including the confidence that his verse will endure, derives from a similarly long tradition.

If there is something unusual in sonnet 18, it is the fact that the subject is described in only the most general terms. The expected "blazon"—or description of the beloved's hair, eyes, lips, face—is omitted. In fact, we learn only that the person is "more lovely and more temperate" than a summer's day, because summer may bring "winds," or the sun may be too hot, or it may be "dimmed."

Although the poem may in this respect be surprising, it nevertheless seems to be rather simple and transparent. Yet, when read in the context of Shakespeare's sequence, its meaning turns out to be radically different from what readers may assume. We soon discover that the sonnet is addressed not to a woman but to a man who is notably superior in social standing to the older poet. Sonnet 18 also comes at a moment when, after the poet has declared his love to the youth, he appears to have received a response of reciprocal affection.

This intricate situation is further complicated by the fact that the poet also hopes to become the "chosen" writer of the youth—a status that is achieved by sonnets 15–17. Sonnet 18 therefore becomes a poem celebrating the young man's beauty, as well as a hymn of triumph in which the poet expresses his feelings of self-fulfillment. A final note: accepting the position of the favored writer plainly implies that the poet is inferior to the youth in social standing, and also (as we will soon learn) in his appearance.

The poet is now implicitly dependent on him in several ways. He must please the friend, and his poetry must continue to be valued by the young man above that of all rivals.

At this point, even more complexities present themselves. Clearly, sonnet 18 is in no sense a spontaneous outpouring of sentiment. Rather, it is carefully constructed to build toward the climactic lines of the final quatrain, with their sudden pivot on the word *but* (line 9) and the following strong assertions reinforced by the repetition "Nor . . . Nor" (lines 10–11). A close analysis would reveal any number of ways in which Shakespeare has masterfully "composed" the poem.

We might, of course, expect no less from any skillful sonneteer. But it is important to note that the poem is in this case not simply a love lyric, but also a sophisticated performance offered to demonstrate the talents of the newly chosen poet. As a result, we should consider whether the opening line is merely a conventional beginning of a poem of praise, or a self-conscious way of asking what kind of sonnet the young man might like: "I can do whatever you prefer: shall I write something that has to do with spring, or would you like a comparison to a summer's day?"

Performance inevitably calls into play some element of manipulation. The poet necessarily assumes a role, and he uses his art to affect his audience—particularly the youth. Moreover, once performance and manipulation enter the scene, it becomes difficult to distinguish between the poetry of genuine feeling—something that is not so easy to define or detect—and that of flattery. For a writer whose friend is expecting serious (or witty) compliments, the poetic challenge is formidable. When is one finding inventive and fresh ways to express one's actual love, and when is one mainly seeking ingenious or familiar methods to celebrate—perhaps extravagantly—someone who is the source of one's heightened status as a chosen writer? The danger of slipping into mere flattery is of course a familiar one in Elizabethan literature, but it reaches greater depths and raises increasingly serious moral questions in

Shakespeare than in any other writer of his time. Indeed, it becomes one of the central themes of the sequence, culminating in the rival poet series (76–86) and in the later sonnets (100–108) that precede the end of the first major section.

Sonnet 18 is also crucial to the poet's own aspirations as an artist, and to the dilemmas created not only by his inferior status but also by his own personal feelings of inadequacy. At this early phase, however, the poet seems fully confident of his capacity to "give life" to the young man, and this confers on him a considerable share of commanding power as well as a greater sense of equality in the relationship. It is true that the beauty and love of the young man are the inspiration for the poet's verse, and the poet is in this sense dependent on him. The youth also retains the ability to act either faithfully and admirably—or far less admirably. He has, in other words, the power to inflict pain, humiliation, and anguish on the poet, since it is the poet who is clearly infatuated, while the young man appears from the beginning to be self-contained and self-absorbed.

In the end, however, the poet has the last word. Only he can choose to immortalize the friend—or not. Only he can choose to characterize the young man as he wishes, and also decide how to represent himself. His verse bestows on him the ability to possess as well as to create. If the poet cannot always depend on the young man's fidelity or his presence, his art affords him a way of sustaining the relationship and, in effect, keeping the youth in his possession.

Finally, in the context of Shakespeare's sequence, "Shall I compare thee" is unusual in both its tone and its style. It is marvelously paced and lucid, especially in the way that its "matter" conforms so thoroughly to the structure of the sonnet form. The iambic meter is undisturbed but not monotonous. There is nothing in the syntax to complicate or distort apparent meaning. The poem moves forward in a measured and effortless way toward the finality of the couplet. Although many poems in Shakespeare's sequence are more powerful, more profound, and more moving than this one, that is very much the point: "Shall I compare thee" expresses precisely what is appropriate at this early stage in the love relationship. Time and Death are momentarily defeated. Love has not yet been tested or blemished. The gold complexion has not yet been dimmed. It is a moment of quiet triumph when everything seems to be within the poet's control, reach, and grasp.

FOUR

Tender Churl

The first seventeen poems of Shakespeare's sequence are often referred to as the "marriage sonnets," essentially because the poet is attempting to persuade a recalcitrant young man—or youth—to marry in order to produce a son and heir. This introduction to the sequence has seemed sufficiently odd to many scholars and critics that several of them have wondered whether the young man's family may have commissioned the poems in order to add yet more ammunition to what had already been expended.

Even if this were true, it would not explain why Shakespeare chose to "reuse" the series, as well as to place it in such a prominent position at the very beginning of so substantial a work. Equally important, the poet's arguments are not at all the conventional ones that would be employed in carrying out an assignment of this kind. The youth is not, for instance, urged to marry in order to preserve his family's name, standing, and presumed wealth. Nor do we find a commandment to procreate—or "increase"—in order to fulfill a religious and moral duty. Instead, the poet's reasons center upon a single point: marriage is necessary in order to ensure that the young man's beauty will survive in the features of a child. As stated in sonnet 4, "Die single, and thine image dies with thee."

This theme signals the poet's clear attraction to the youth, and these opening sonnets inevitably raise the question of how the poet will proceed—and how the young man will respond to any overtures by the poet, however discreet. Will he be flattered, indifferent, or even repulsed? Moreover, given the poet's energetic and quite continuous criticism (as well as praise) of the young man—who refuses to give himself in marriage—how should we interpret the tone of these poems? Should we read the poet's "assaults" as examples of his extraordinary inventiveness and wit—performances meant to surprise and entertain the young man with arguments and sudden parries or thrusts that are well within the rules of the game? Or do they sometimes hit home with considerable force, in ways that are unexpected and disconcerting—intended to provoke as much as to persuade?

In the very first sonnet, the young man is described as a "tender churl" who makes "waste in niggarding." Shortly after, he is a "glutton" who eats "the world's due." Elsewhere, he is an "unthrift" whose beauty, if kept "unused," will be "destroyed." In sonnet 4, the young man spends his "legacy" of beauty only upon himself, rather than marrying and providing the world with a son. In fact, he is warned that Nature "gives nothing"—she only lends,

> And being frank she lends to those are free:
> Then, beauteous niggard, why dost thou abuse
> The bounteous largess given thee to give?

(4)

The youth hoards for himself, or else spends what he ought generously to give to others. Freely given and unforced love, as well as constancy in love, are two of the central themes of the entire sequence, and they begin to make their significance felt—almost in passing—at this early stage in the work.

Even the poet's critique in sonnet 4 might pass without undue notice if he did not become increasingly pointed and impassioned as the series progresses. At moments, he verges on forceful accusation or attack, and this drive culminates in sonnets 9 and 10. Here, the poet declares that "No love toward others in that bosom sits /

That on himself such murd'rous shame commits" (9). This accusation is then repeated (twice) in sonnet 10, and becomes even more insistent:

> For shame deny that thou bear'st love to any,
> Who for thy self art so unprovident.
> Grant, if thou wilt, thou art beloved of many,
> But that thou none lov'st is most evident;
> For thou art so possessed with murd'rous hate,
> That 'gainst thy self thou stick'st not to conspire . . .
>
> (10)

The lines are awkward, but their ineloquent bluntness suits the poet's shift into declarative plain-speaking. The refrain—that the youth loves no one—runs through both sonnets 9 and 10, and the "murd'rous shame" of sonnet 9 is heightened to "murd'rous hate" in 10.

For the first time, we are also made aware of a more public realm—a larger and also nearby world in which the young man is apparently "beloved of many" and yet cannot (or refuses to) love anyone in return. Moreover, there is now an implied or actual conversation taking place between the poet and the youth. In effect, the poet says that he will "grant, if you wish, that many people love you, but that does not change the fact that you love only yourself."

These lines can be read simply as a continuation of the poet's attempt to urge marriage on the young man, but they are expressed with a greater sense of urgency, approaching a personal plea for some clear response. In fact, this becomes explicit in the last lines of the sonnet:

> O change thy thought, that I may change my mind!
> Shall hate be fairer lodged than gentle love?
> Be as thy presence is, gracious and kind,
> Or to thy self at least kind-hearted prove:

Make thee another self for love of me,
That beauty still may live in thine or thee.

(10)

The young man is asked to change his "thought"—to marry and procreate; to be "gracious and kind"; and perhaps to begin to return the poet's love. This plea is then followed by the poet's desire that the change will be made "for love of me." The last line of the sonnet may press matters even further, introducing a note of potential ambiguity: the youth's beauty *may* be preserved by a child—"thine"—but also, perhaps, by the young man himself ("or thee"). The idea is not further elaborated, but perhaps another path forward (not simply procreation) may be available, possibly through the poet's own "eternal lines."

Having pressed so hard and so personally, the poet momentarily steps back, returning to the marriage theme. But by sonnet 13 he is addressing the youth forthrightly as "love"; in 14, the eyes of the young man (or friend) are the poet's "constant stars" from which he derives all his "knowledge"; and by 15, the poet—presumably encouraged by the friend—decides to conquer Time's reputed power over beauty: "And all in war with Time for love of you, / As he takes from you, I engraft you new."

Now the poet's verse will renew or preserve the youth's beauty, and it is clear that the young man has to some extent returned the poet's expressions of affection. In addition, we learn that the poet has apparently become the youth's favored writer. In the first lines of sonnet 16, the poet wonders why the friend has not decided to rely on something "mightier" than the poet's "barren rhyme" in order to defend himself against the ravages of Time: he suggests that the birth of a child "Can make you live yourself." But the issue has essentially been resolved. While the very end of sonnet 17 refers once again to "some child of yours," the poem as a whole celebrates the youth's beauty and the last line makes clear that the young man—in any event—lives "in my rhyme." The whole of sonnet 18 ("Shall I compare thee") then settles the entire matter conclusively.

In short, the young man has now "chosen" the poet; the young man and the poet appear to have expressed some reciprocity in love; and all thought of the friend's undertaking a conventional marriage has vanished. The hope now—at least on the part of the poet—is whether there may instead be a metaphorical "marriage" of some kind.

•

In retrospect, we can see why the marriage sonnets provided the poet with the kind of introduction to the sequence that he required. He could hardly have started in the way that virtually all such works begin—with explicit poems of praise and declarations of love, as well as with a traditional description of the beloved's features. Rather, he needed an oblique approach as he tried to discover—or provoke—an expression of the youth's feelings toward him. He also needed a theme that would allow him to celebrate the young man and his beauty, while also enabling him to move carefully, step by discreet step, before revealing his own strong affection.

In the process, the poet created a preliminary sketch of his friend's character. In the first few sonnets, he found himself resorting to easy oxymorons and similar terms to describe the youth— *tender churl, beauteous niggard, beauty's waste*—complimenting the friend while simultaneously criticizing him. In general, the terms focused considerably on the youth's profligacy as well as his niggardliness or selfishness. By the time we reach the sonnets that are central to this group, the main stress is on the young man's inability to love, in spite of the fact that he enjoys the love of so many others. He is self-enclosed, and this raises an inevitable question about the extent of his actual affection for the poet: how fixed or firm is it, and how genuinely mutual is the love between the two figures? The apparent reciprocity that led to the creation of "Shall I compare thee" seemed much more than merely ritual-istic, but the actual situation was nevertheless unclear. Meanwhile, the poet's infatuation with the friend (and with his new favored status) inevitably causes him to set aside—indeed, to overlook, at least temporarily—those qualities of the youth that seem least admirable. The young man now appears to be "gracious and kind" and "more lovely and more temperate" (10, 18).

•

It would be misleading to pass over this set of sonnets without commenting on those concerned with Time the destroyer, espe-cially since Time plays such a major role in several important sections of Shakespeare's entire sequence. The best of the early sonnets on Time (5, 12, 15, 18) are tender and lyrical in their sensi-tivity and in their capacity to evoke—with delicate imagery—the nature of the changing seasons. In general, these poems avoid the high conquistadorial rhetoric of sonnets such as 55 ("Not marble nor the gilded monuments / Of princes shall outlive this pow'rful rhyme"). Instead, there is generally a quiet confidence that Time can be defeated despite its seeming relentlessness and omni-potence: the young man's beauty can be rescued, if not through the likeness of a son, then more prominently through the poet's verse.

Later in the sequence, there is less confidence that this can be achieved. The inevitability of eventual loss (in 60, 63–65, 104, 108, 126), as well as the poet's own approaching death (in 73), is inti-mated. Finally, in sonnets 100 and 104, there are concerns about the effect that the passing of Time may be having on the friend; and in several other important poems (115, 116, 123, 124) the poet contends directly with Time in the hope of overcoming its powers. For the moment, however, we see in the marriage sonnets a full awareness of Time's threat, combined with a conviction that it can be thwarted:

When I consider every thing that grows
Holds in perfection but a little moment,

TENDER CHURL

That this huge stage presenteth nought but shows
Whereon the stars in secret influence comment;
When I perceive that men as plants increase,
Cheered and checked even by the selfsame sky,
Vaunt in their youthful sap, at height decrease,
And wear their brave state out of memory:
Then the conceit of this inconstant stay
Sets you most rich in youth before my sight,
Where wasteful Time debateth with Decay
To change your day of youth to sullied night;
   And all in war with Time for love of you,
   As he takes from you, I engraft you new.

(15)

FIVE

Master-Mistress

Sonnet 20 is one of the pivotal poems in the sequence. The poet feels prompted to explain the nature and intensity of his love. In the process, he resorts to a form of wit and mock-mythology that—especially in the poem's last line—raises as many questions as it answers. This complexity has led some critics to see the poet's love as a plea to the young man for a powerful mutual friendship devoid of any physical or sexual desire. Others have viewed the relationship as homoerotic, and some have described it as explicitly homosexual.

Half a century ago, Richard Blackmur characterized the poet's state as one of infatuation—as a set of emotions that includes a clear element of desire; an impulse to idealize the beloved; and a feeling of riveted magnetic attraction that drives the poet to forgive the young man's faults and successive infidelities. In effect, the poet's imagination has created a vision of love that beguiles and overwhelms him: a vision that is more than once shattered, but is so powerful that the poet continually attempts to re-create and sustain it, in spite of continual betrayals.

In sonnet 20, the main conceit involves a sudden and unexpected transmutation:

A woman's face with Nature's own hand painted
Hast thou, the master-mistress of my passion;

A woman's gentle heart, but not acquainted
With shifting change, as is false women's fashion;
An eye more bright than theirs, less false in rolling,
Gilding the object whereupon it gazeth;
A man in hue, all hues in his controlling,
Which steals men's eyes and women's souls amazeth.

(20)

The young man is presented as having many of the characteristics of a woman, although by the fourth line (and then more explicitly in the seventh) he is no less a man. He "steals men's eyes" and "amazes" those of women. And although he is a man in "hue"—a complex word that may be defined to mean appearance—he "controls" (or has power over) all other hues, whether those of men or women. Indeed, he is the poet's "master-mistress": a ruling figure to whom the poet has made himself subject and, simultaneously, a "woman" with whom the poet has fallen in love:

And for a woman wert thou first created,
Till Nature as she wrought thee fell a-doting,
And by addition me of thee defeated,
By adding one thing to my purpose nothing.
But since she prick'd thee out for women's pleasure,
Mine be thy love, and thy love's use their treasure.

(20)

The poet is on the brink of possession when Nature—also doting on the youth—transforms "her" to a man by "pricking" her out in order to enjoy her for her own pleasure. The poet is thwarted and, in effect, cheated by a form of fate. His physical desires are frustrated, without necessarily being fully extinguished. Transfixed by love, he explains his predicament by suggesting—with obvious wit—that he has been overpowered by forces beyond his control. Given this situation, he asks (in the last line) for the youth's commit ment to an ideal of mutual love, while acknowledging that the young man's sexual "use" (and "treasure") will be reserved for women.

This apparently easy division between "love" and "love's use" seems to resolve the poem, at least rhetorically. It suggests, however, that the poet will be able to accept the young man's liberties without difficulty—so long as the commitment to mutual love between the poet and the youth is sustained. This presumption proves, of course, to be far from possible. The poet's love is too deeply passionate to withstand—without shock—any form of transgression on the part of the young man; and the young man's susceptibility to temptation is so great that it inevitably impinges on his ability to maintain the strength of his commitment to the poet.

Sonnet 20 is a poem that was inevitable. The poet's professions of love have been so strong and deep that they effectively called for some explanation at this point in the sequence, even if the explanation was "mythological," partly witty, and ultimately evasive. There was some need on the part of the poet to try to clear the air, or to describe the nature of his complex predicament, and to propose a possible resolution in the form of a committed "mutual" love. Yet, in the end, the sonnet remains unresolved, essentially because the poet's conflicting feelings and emotions are themselves unresolved. His love idealizes the youth, but also contains an element of desire that cannot now be satisfied. The poet is consigned to an existence in which his own devotion to the friend—and his poetry of praise—are constantly undermined by the young man's free "use" of the "treasure" he bestows upon others. Feelings of jealousy, bitterness, self-pity, self-abnegation, and accusation soon lead the poet to create verse that is very different from sonnet 18 (as well as many other celebratory poems in the sequence). Only in the very last phase of the sonnets to the friend is there a marked change, when a different conception of love—and a different style—emerge.

SIX

Outcast State

As we move to the next group of sonnets (21–32), we find not a carefully plotted series, but a change in the landscape and the interior weather of the poems. Following the first twenty sonnets, we expect the poet to explore ways in which to praise and compliment the young man, relying to some extent on familiar aspects of the sonnet tradition while altering and shaping them to suit his own purposes. And so he does. But the changes are at times less lyrical in nature than they are disruptive. Indeed, the poet often dwells on his own inadequacies—his age, his looks, his "outcast state," and the apparent inferiority of his verse when compared with that of others. He wonders, therefore, whether the young man is in fact committed to him, or whether he will be swept aside. Because he is uncertain of his status, some of his poems of praise seem ambiguous, others express apprehensions, and some emphasize the great gap in social standing that separates him so dramatically from the young man.

At the very beginning of this group, sonnet 22 opens with the poet's preoccupation with his age, and then offers an ingenious solution to dispose of the disparity between him and the youth: since the poet's heart resides in the young man's breast, he possesses, in effect, all the "beauty that doth cover"—or belongs to—the youth. Given this fact, the poet asks, "How can I then be elder than thou art?" But this use of mock-logic does not dispel the poet's anxiety, and the final six lines of the sonnet find him imploring the young man to be as careful or "wary" in bearing the poet's heart as the poet will be in return. Indeed, the poet claims that he will guard the friend's heart like "a tender nurse," and the friend should do the same, remaining true to the terms of their original, mutual commitment:

> Presume not on thy heart when mine is slain;
> Thou gav'st me thine not to give back again.

(22)

The sudden thrust of the last line lays bare the fear that has existed from the poem's beginning. The friend may change his mind—take back his heart—and break the relationship, perhaps to seek someone more youthful and more beauteous.

Once made explicit, this possibility affects the reading of other apparently uncomplicated sonnets in this group. In 24, for example, the poet is said to have painted the friend's image—lodged in the poet's breast—so perfectly that even the sun delights to gaze on it. Yet the poet has only the ability or "cunning" to present a picture of the friend's *exterior* beauty, nothing beyond: his eyes "draw . . . what they see, know not the heart." In an apparently charming and complimentary sonnet, is there a sudden reversal at the end—an expression of doubt about the friend's fidelity? Or is the line quite innocent, indicating that if one knew the heart, it would reveal itself to be entirely constant?

Anxiety about the possible loss of the friend tends to merge with concerns about the adequacy of the poet's verse—including fears that the young man will find it wanting. And this leads in turn to a deeper question: what form of praise would best represent sincerity of feeling and the depths of a powerful love? The very first poem of this kind (21) offers a witty, flippant reply to such a question. The poet will not indulge in extravagant similes and other figures of speech, and will not resort to falsely "painted beauty" or other forms of flattery: "I will not praise that purpose not to sell." The possibility and danger of flattery; the presence of other poets willing to sell their wares; and the declared intention to be accurate and plain-speaking in one's praise all converge in this slight poem that nevertheless provides an introduction to a major, continuing theme throughout the sequence.

That theme is developed very soon, in sonnet 23, where the poet, in attempting to speak, experiences a form of stage fright, like "an unperfect actor on the stage, / Who with his fear is put beside his part." In this case, it is partly the poet's fear of his "audience" and its response to his "performance," and partly the actual power and depth of his love—indeed, its scarcely controlled "rage"—that cripple his ability to express his feelings in a "perfect ceremony of love's rite." The alternative to the poet's halting speech is a form of silence, but one that can be atoned for in "books"—in poems—that "plead for love, and look for recompense" in the form of reciprocal affection. Other poets may be able to speak with apparent eloquence; the friend, however, is asked to read what silent love has written, and to "hear with eyes" what "love's fine wit" has composed. Indeed, he is explicitly asked to ignore other writers whose "tongues" may have spoken in words of extravagant praise.

The sonnet is striking, and some of the most revealing lines are those in which the poet's stage fright compels his silence, moving him to plead for the friend's love in response. Here, as much as anywhere, we experience the poet's helplessness, as well as the young man's power to give or to withhold. At one level, this drama is a purely personal one between the two protagonists. At another level, however, it is a metaphor for the very idea of performance, for the theater, and for art—as well as for the ultimate dependence of actors (or poets) and their "productions" on the response of their audiences.

This becomes even clearer if sonnet 23 is compared with its close analogue in *A Midsummer Night's Dream*. There, Bottom and his amateur, clownish "mechanics" present *Pyramus and Thisby* (a play of "very tragical mirth") to Duke Theseus, Queen Hippolyta, and their retinue. Hippolyta is brusque and impatient with the entertainment ("This is the silliest thing I ever saw") while Theseus is sympathetic and indulgent, as well as condescending and rather mocking: "Our sport will be to enjoy the mistakes of the actors." Hippolyta is urged to overlook the foolishness of the players: even the best of them, after all, "are but shadows; and the worst are no worse, if imagination amend them."

The complexity and variety of these "audience responses" suggest why "unperfect" actors such as the poet in sonnet 23 are inevitably apprehensive. They are in one sense "nothing"—mere shadows—compelled to play roles for the pleasure of others, and subject to the scorn (as well as possible approval) of those who look on. At the very least, they are always in need of some indulgence. When Hippolyta challenges Theseus's willingness to view Bottom and his company sympathetically, he replies that he has often been met by "clerks" who have come to bring formal greetings to him, and has seen them

> . . . shiver and look pale,
> Make periods in the midst of sentences,
> Throttle their polish'd accent in their fears,
> And in conclusion, dumbly have broke off,
> Not paying me a welcome.
>
> (V, i, 95–99)

Instead of betraying anger, Theseus understands that "out of this silence" a welcome had been intended, and he "reads" as much from this "modesty of fearful duty" as from any "rattling tongue" who offers him merely "saucy and audacious eloquence." He prefers, as he says, an expression of "love" and "tongue-tied simplicity" to a barrage of inflated rhetoric: those who speak "least" actually "speak most."

While Theseus suggests how one ought to respond, the poet

of the Sonnets is simply left with the hope that the youth may perhaps "learn to read what silent love hath writ," but there is no assurance. His pleading suggests his deep concern about the possible fragility of the love relationship, as well as his status as favored poet. In particular, there is also the implication that potential rivals may offer (as Theseus said) "saucy and audacious eloquence," saying more with their "tongues" than the poet has been able to express (23, line 12). In other words, this sonnet extends the subject of poetic rivalry beyond its brief introduction in sonnet 21: it is now becoming a preoccupation of the poet, foreshadowing the rival poet series as well as later sonnets.

The next poem that deals with the question of poetic praise and style—as well as the poet's dilemma—is sonnet 26. It is in many respects a curious poem. Its form of address is unexpected:

> Lord of my love, to whom in vassalage
> Thy merit hath my duty strongly knit,
> To thee I send this written ambassage
> To witness duty, not to show my wit;
> Duty so great, which wit so poor as mine
> May make seem bare, in wanting words to show it,
> But that I hope some good conceit of thine
> In thy soul's thought (all naked) will bestow it . . .
>
> (26)

This "letter" to the friend is a sonnet of praise par excellence, where the poet's purported want of wit and words is actually a way of complimenting the young man: only some "good conceit" or idea of the youth can rescue the poet and enable him to express—with eloquence—his duty and his love.

But the exceptional formality of the tone is unusual (even for a message in an epistolary style): there is the considerable distance introduced by the lord/vassal language, by the continued emphasis on duty, and by the use of terms such as *merit, ambassage,* and *respect.*

The voice we hear is quite new in Shakespeare's sequence, and it suggests a greater sense of accepted subordination and self-isolation than we have heard before. In addition, the last lines of the sonnet indicate that, until the friend intervenes, the poet will remain in a form of hiding or self-exile; only when the young man grants him the fine "apparel" necessary to clothe his verse will he be able to

> . . . dare to boast how I do love thee;
> Till then, not show my head where thou mayst prove me.
>
> (26)

This conclusion may be read as pure praise (or flattery?). But the poet's reticence even to "show my head" and declare his love is disconcerting, as is his feeling that, if left to himself, he and his verse will be tested and found wanting: the friend may "prove" him.

It is a long step—but nevertheless only a step—from the lord/vassal language and sense of subordination in sonnet 26 to the language and situation of sonnets 57–58, where the poet, alone, has been deserted by the young man, and has been reduced to a state of far greater dependence. Now his only defense against complete humiliation is bitterness that takes the form of fierce irony:

> That god forbid, that made me first your slave,
> I should in thought control your times of pleasure,
> Or at your hand th'account of hours to crave,
> Being your vassal bound to stay your leisure.
>
> (58)

And later:

> But my five wits nor my five senses can
> Dissuade one foolish heart from serving thee,
> Who leaves unswayed the likeness of a man,
> Thy proud heart's slave and vassal wretch to be.
>
> (141)

Sonnets 29 and 30 represent the culmination of this series. Both are meditations: in 30, a train of memories and regrets; in 29, a reflection upon the poet's desires, wishes, and hopes. In one, the poet is overcome by the recollection of what has been lost; in the other, by vivid reminders of what he has never possessed:

> When in disgrace with Fortune and men's eyes,
> I all alone beweep my outcast state,
> And trouble deaf heaven with my bootless cries,
> And look upon myself and curse my fate,
> Wishing me like to one more rich in hope,
> Featured like him, like him with friends possessed,
> Desiring this man's art, and that man's scope,
> With what I most enjoy contented least;
> Yet in these thoughts myself almost despising . . .

> (29)

The lines highlight, in concentrated form, many of the anxieties and inadequacies that the poet has previously expressed. He wishes that he were "featured like him"; he envies the art and talent—as well as the scope, hope, and friends—of others. Not only is he in disgrace with Fortune, but also with "men's eyes." He is seen as somehow tainted, and he feels alienated, expelled, "outcast."

Once again, however, he shifts the blame to others. Earlier, in sonnet 20, he found Nature guilty of depriving him of the young man; here, "fate" is responsible for his plight. Fortune has repudiated him, and heaven is "deaf" to his cries. Doomed, he "all alone beweeps" his state, and comes "almost" to despise himself.

If the poet now seems more isolated than ever, he suddenly changes course:

> Yet in these thoughts myself almost despising,
> Haply I think on thee, and then my state
> (Like to the lark at break of day arising
> From sullen earth) sings hymns at heaven's gate,

For thy sweet love rememb'red such wealth brings
That then I scorn to change my state with kings.

(29)

The poet's catalogue of complaints had reached a point of no return—"With what I most enjoy contented least." There is no discernible exit from the world in which he finds himself, except to discover another realm in which all might be, as if magically, transformed. "Thinking on" the friend and his presumed love for the poet brings about this swift mutation. The "sullen earth" is left behind; the cries to "deaf heaven" are replaced by "hymns at heaven's gate"; and the poet's outcast state is enriched with un-expected wealth—a new "state" superior to that of kings.

At this point, however, the new realm is one of the imagina-tion, created when the poet is alone, without access to what the young man may be thinking. He remembers the friend's "sweet love," but by this stage in the sequence, we know that the poet has some misgivings if not serious doubts about the constancy of the youth's love. We realize—once again, but now more vividly—how great is the chasm in status and good fortune between the two men, and how much the poet's entire existence can be changed, for better or worse, by the friend. The friend makes, quite liter-ally, all the difference between the poet's isolated life "in dis-grace," or his place—as chosen writer—in a sphere where his very being is transformed.

SEVEN

Thy Advocate

In sonnets 21–31, there have been intimations that the poet's commitment to the love relationship was deeper than that of the friend. The poet could draw the friend's features with accuracy, but could not see what lay in his heart; and while the poet's own heart was "slain," it was not at all clear that the friend's was equally so: "Thou gav'st me thine not to give back again" (22).

These and similar forebodings prove to have been only too accurate. In sonnet 33, the poet has been suddenly deserted by the youth, who simply disappears. But in view of the poet's earlier doubts and fears, the desertion is perhaps less surprising than the poet's response to it, not only in sonnet 33 but also in 34–36. There we find individual reactions to what has taken place, as well as a distinctive pattern of successive responses that will be repeated elsewhere in the sequence. The pattern (if not always identical) illuminates the qualities and character of the young man, and—even more powerfully—those of the poet. It contributes to our knowledge of the cyclical, "trapped" nature of the experiences in which both protagonists find themselves—as well as to the progressive forward movement of "sentiments" that Blackmur noted.

Once the young friend has left, the poet's reaction in sonnet 33 is complex. His initial characterization of the youth (and of the entire situation) is ambivalent. He first describes the events in terms of the real celestial sun (or "sovereign eye"), which becomes, by implication, an extended metaphor for the friend and his behavior:

Full many a glorious morning have I seen
Flatter the mountain tops with sovereign eye,
Kissing with golden face the meadows green,
Gilding pale streams with heavenly alchemy;
Anon permit the basest clouds to ride
With ugly rack on his celestial face,
And from the forlorn world his visage hide,
Stealing unseen to west with this disgrace . . .

(33)

The clouds are described in human moral terms and the sun portrayed as a victim. The "basest clouds" ride with "ugly rack" across the sun, hiding his "disgraced" face from the forlorn world. The dark clouds are the obvious guilty parties. The sun remains helpless, and has been passive throughout; the "aggressive" other phenomena are to blame for all that has happened.

This scene is then repeated more succinctly in the next lines. The sun is again cast as victim—with an explicit reference to the friend: "Even so my sun one early morn did shine." Yet the poet's piercing cry—"he was but one hour mine"—contains no direct accusation of the young man, and the following line extends the aggressor-victim metaphor further: "The region cloud hath masked him from me now." Only in the couplet does it become clear that the poet holds the friend responsible:

Yet him for this my love no whit disdaineth:
Suns of the world may stain, when heaven's sun staineth.

(33)

The sun (or friend) has either "stained" himself or allowed himself to be stained by others. A real sun may be dimmed or blighted by clouds in a perfectly natural way, but a human "sun" or sovereign, in spite of the tempting analogy, clearly bears responsibility for whatever has happened. Meanwhile, the poet claims—with irony—that he does not "disdain" the young man.

44

The poet's feelings are clearly divided. He has a strong initial inclination to protect the young man from any taint. Even his condemnation, in the couplet, is not plainly accusatory. He may not yet have been able to absorb the full sense of shock, and he may be reluctant to react aggressively because the young man's desertion may prove to be only temporary. The relationship matters to the poet absolutely, and he is unwilling—indeed unable—to give up the love that essentially tyrannizes him and binds him so irrevocably to the youth.

In sonnets 34 and 35, a reunion of the two men takes place, but as these poems (including 36) unfold, they begin to reveal the pattern—just mentioned—that will be repeated later in the sequence. Meanwhile, sonnet 34 initially continues the sun-cloud metaphor of 33, but uses it for quite different purposes:

Why didst thou promise such a beauteous day,
And make me travel forth without my cloak,
To let base clouds o'ertake me in my way,
Hiding thy brav'ry in their rotten smoke?
'Tis not enough that through the cloud thou break,
To dry the rain on my storm-beaten face,
For no man well of such a salve can speak,
That heals the wound, and cures not the disgrace:
Nor can thy shame give physic to my grief;
Though thou repent, yet I have still the loss . . .

(34)

In contrast to sonnet 33, the poet openly criticizes the young man's offense (once again assuming the role of victim). He was promised something "beauteous" in love and was "made"—compelled—to travel confidently, without defenses, only to discover that the friend has betrayed him, deliberately confounding him in the process. The poet's catalogue of self-pitying grievances, though objectively justifiable, nevertheless suggests his weakness and intense vulnerability. He is once again in "disgrace." Even the "repentance" of the friend does not compensate for the "loss" the poet has visibly suffered.

From a rhetorical point of view, the litany proves effective and produces the only response that seems adequate to the poet:

> Th'offender's sorrow lends but weak relief
> To him that bears the strong offence's cross.
>   Ah, but those tears are pearl which thy love sheeds,
>   And they are rich, and ransom all ill deeds.
>
> (34)

The friend is contrite and sorrowful: he returns to the poet and spontaneously weeps—a rich ransom of pearls that serves to "pay for" his ill deeds. The affection of the young man seems genuine, though the tears appear to flow easily, making it difficult to judge the depth of the source from which they spring. But the breach appears to be resolved, however temporarily.

At the beginning of sonnet 35, the poet suggests that the friend should no longer "be grieved at that which thou hast done." All beautiful things are said to have the germ of their own infection within them ("Roses have thorns . . . And loathsome canker lives in sweetest bud"); indeed,

> All men make faults, and even I in this,
> Authorising thy trespass with compare,
> My self corrupting salving thy amiss,
> Excusing thy sins more than their sins are;
> For to thy sensual fault I bring in sense . . .
>
> (35)

When the poet equates nature's flaws with the moral failings of human beings, he clearly betrays himself: he has implicitly excused—too easily—the friend's trespass, and the excusal amounts to a form of self-corruption. We now learn that the young man's fault was a "sensual"—presumably sexual—one; his transgression may be pardoned, but that is obviously different from defending it with "sense" or reason:

Thy adverse party is thy advocate—
And 'gainst myself a lawful plea commence:
Such civil war is in my love and hate
    That I an accessory needs must be
    To that sweet thief which sourly robs from me.

                                  (35)

The poet is now in the paradoxical position of arguing against his own sense of what is morally right. He is an "accessory" to the friend's crime, essentially because his love is so strong that it compels him to be an accomplice. Meanwhile, the young man has become a "sweet thief" who robs the poet, not only of his moral standing but also of his previous faith in an untainted reciprocal love between himself and the youth. Both the friend and the poet are now guilty of serious betrayals—one of them sensual, and the other rooted in reason. Reunion has created something less than a full reconciliation: an uncertain state that may well make other failures more likely. Nevertheless, love has in fact been reaffirmed, and this accomplishment points to the possibility of other reaffirmations in the future.

    The final sonnet (36) in this group seems a strange departure from the previous three. The poet declares that he and the friend must separate—"be twain"—not because the relationship has been bruised or crippled beyond repair, nor because the friend's transgression is unforgivable, but because of the poet's own "blots" and ill-repute:

I may not evermore acknowledge thee,
Lest my bewailed guilt should do thee shame,
Nor thou with public kindness honour me,
Unless thou take that honour from thy name:
    But do not so; I love thee in such sort,
    As thou being mine, mine is thy good report.

                                  (36)

It is not unusual for the poet to dwell on his own inadequacy, questioning whether he is a source of embarrassment (rather than an ornament) in his relationship with the friend. But at this particular moment the shift is at first puzzling: why should the burden of guilt be entirely the poet's? First, the poet seems to be seeking reassurance that the reunion (in 34) has been genuine. Following his accusations of the friend, as well as his assertions of self-corruption in 35, he looks for an unambiguous signal from the youth. His announcement of a need to separate, therefore, seems to be offered primarily in the hope of being contradicted. Indeed, in the last line, he continues to think of the love relationship as fundamentally unchanged: "thou being mine."

But the unexpected shift in sonnet 36 also seems intrinsic: the poet cannot overcome his own deep feelings of shame and inferiority, which rise to the surface continuously throughout the sequence, as if he were forced to repent for having accused the friend so directly—or even for having provoked the restoration of the relationship so insistently. A strange form of guilt, together with a continuing sense of inadequacy, leads him to assume the blame for all that has happened. In the process, self-accusation becomes an inverted form of praise.

What we experience in sonnets 33–36 is the pattern mentioned earlier. It involves a betrayal by the friend, followed by accusations from the poet that lead to a reconciliation; then to feelings of guilt and unworthiness on the part of the poet, accompanied by a proposed separation (in the hope that the separation will be rejected); and finally to a continuation of the relationship, in spite of all that has happened. The friend remains invincibly self-secure, whatever his offenses; and the poet considers himself to be tainted or infectious. Such are the convolutions of feeling and action that come to mark several of the most significant episodes in the entire sequence.

EIGHT

Usurpation

The sonnets from 37 to 42 focus primarily on the second major shock of the sequence—the action of the friend in gaining possession of the poet's mistress. Early intimations appear in sonnets 37–39, where the two men continue their separation ("let us divided live") following the farewell in 36 ("we two must be twain"). Although the friend's betrayal in 40–42 seems at first to be simply another offense by the young man, it has deeper implications both for an understanding of the youth and for the nature of the relationship between the two main figures. In the process, it helps to clarify how the sequence will develop in its incidents and themes.

Sonnet 40 opens abruptly, as if an immediate reaction to a sudden—but half-expected—discovery:

> Take all my loves, my love, yea take them all;
> What hast thou then more than thou hadst before?
> No love, my love, that thou mayst true love call,
> All mine was thine, before thou hadst this more.
> Then if for my love thou my love receivest,
> I cannot blame thee, for my love thou usest;
> But yet be blamed, if thou this self deceivest . . .

(40)

The assumption is that the poet and friend are in effect "one" ("All mine was thine, before thou hadst this more"). A number of changes are then wrung upon the word *love*—whose meaning now includes the poet, the friend, the mistress, and the concept of love itself. Elucidating the syntax of the opening few lines is important, but no more so than noting the vast difference in tone between this poem and those written at the time of the friend's first offense. From the start, we hear a voice that is—in spite of the situation—ironic, almost world-weary, as if the poet were by now less surprised and more prepared for another disruptive event: "Take all my loves, my love, yea take them all." The lines that follow, however, are compacted and tightly controlled, suggesting the deep feelings of loss that lie beneath the witty wordplay—in which *my, me, mine, thou, thee, thy, thine, love, my love, no love,* and *true love* are separated and yet interrelated through the poem's grammatical density. Repetitions and variations combine with a form of logic to suggest that the complexity of the poet's emotions depends on the sonnet's linguistic intricacy in order to find the means to express themselves.

By now, the poet knows the youth and himself so well that there is no expectation of a confession from the young man. It is the poet who moves with obvious irony to forgive what has happened, despite the fact that he has had to endure love's (not hate's) "wrong." Meanwhile, he describes the young man both as a "gentle thief" and as a personification of "lascivious grace"—presenting him as paradoxical in nature—a youth whose glistening beauty serves primarily as a cover for his wantonness:

> I do forgive thy robb'ry, gentle thief,
> Although thou steal thee all my poverty;
> And yet love knows it is a greater grief
> To bear love's wrong than hate's known injury.
>> Lascivious grace, in whom all ill well shows,
>> Kill me with spites; yet we must not be foes.

(40)

Regardless of the level of "ill" or corruption that may lie within him, the youth remains beguilingly beauteous, "gentle," and gracious—qualities that bind the poet to him. Indeed, in the final line, the poet's passion makes itself so deeply felt that it overcomes all other considerations: better to be the victim of a deliberately injurious act than to surrender the relationship: "yet we must not be foes."

By the next sonnet (41), the poet is ready to offer a rationale (and an excuse) for the young man's actions. His failings are "pretty wrongs that liberty commits / When I am sometime absent from thy heart." The youth is viewed—with irony—as at least partly faithful: only "sometime" betraying the poet's heart. But in the final lines, the poet makes clear that the implications are far more serious:

> Ay me, but yet thou mightst my seat forbear,
> And chide thy beauty, and thy straying youth,
> Who lead thee in their riot even there
> Where thou art forced to break a twofold truth:
> > Hers, by thy beauty tempting her to thee,
> > Thine, by thy beauty being false to me.

(41)

There is an initial slight effort here to suggest that the young man's actions are not entirely under his control: his beauty and his youth "lead" him astray. But this line of argument is quickly abandoned, and his transgression is recognized as an act of "riot." Indeed, the poet has already been altogether explicit: "Ay me, but yet thou mightst my seat forbear." Here, the poet insists that he has suffered an act of dispossession and usurpation, a forceful stripping away of power—his "seat"—in relationship to the mistress.

The theme of usurpation or dispossession recurs throughout the Sonnets, often as an undercurrent rather than something altogether explicit. As such, it resembles similar themes in several of Shakespeare's plays written near the turn of the century: *Measure for Measure, Henry IV, Hamlet,* and—somewhat earlier—*Richard II.*

In *Richard*, the king is successively divested of his armies, his close courtiers, his crown, his queen, and—symbolically, as a final humiliation—his "seat" upon "roan Barbery," the king's steed, which Bollingbroke "usurps" (V, v, 89). Indeed, the Sonnets can be seen, in part, as a sketch for such tales (with *Lear* as the obvious paradigm). The poet first loses the youth (in 20), when Nature deprives him of "her" by transforming her into a young man. Next he loses the friend ("he was but one hour mine"), who is stolen by unknown "base" others (33). Then he strips himself of his own moral standing through self-corruption (35), and finally the mistress is willfully stolen from him. Later in the sequence, the poet suffers even greater losses. In addressing the dark lady near the end of the sequence, he asks:

> Is't not enough to torture me alone,
> But slave to slavery my sweet'st friend must be?
> Me from myself thy cruel eye hath taken,
> And my next self thou harder hast engrossed;
> Of him, myself, and thee I am forsaken . . .
>
> (133)

The final poem of this group (42) focuses—with witty but perverse logic—on the poet's efforts to both excuse and condemn the friend and the mistress. The friend, he stresses, is the greater loss, although by the sonnet's last line he "rejoices" that, given the mock-logic of the poem, the mistress actually "loves but me alone." This "argument," however, is transparently problematic. In reality, the poet has lost "both twain," and they in turn have laid "on me this cross." Indeed, a distinctive characteristic of the poem emerges as the poet begins to define the relationship between himself and both his "loving offenders":

> Thou dost love her because thou know'st I love her,
> And for my sake even so doth she abuse me . . .
>
> (42)

The first line may appear benign ("You inevitably feel that you ought to love her as a gesture of friendship, because you know how much I love her"), but the actual tone is bitter: "You have decided to love her and take her from me, precisely because you know how much pain this will inflict on me." The mistress has also "abused" him. Both lovers understand the extent of their power over the poet. The youth's betrayal of the poet had been primarily spontaneous, but he also seems to have acted with considerable self-consciousness, taking pleasure in the poet's helplessness. The poet, in turn, not only accepts the injury but condones it, following the pattern described in 33–36. He assumes the role of victim and vassal because he sees no alternative: "Kill me with spites . . ." (40).

This pattern—a form of sadism on the part of the young man (and of the mistress), matched with a form of masochism on the part of the poet—begins to provide much of the energy that drives the sequence and also helps to explain the continuation of the love relationship through its many collapses and recoveries. The role that each of the two central figures plays depends on that of the other. They are locked in a cycle of repetitive actions and reactions driven by the distortions of passion, creating a strange equilibrium from a radical disequilibrium.

Other elements that may help to sustain the relationship include the friend's vanity and his desire to retain an extraordinary poet capable of satisfying his desire for praise and amusement. The poet, for his part, hopes to continue his role as the young man's chosen writer and friend—a role that rescues him from his outcast state. But these factors alone could certainly not in themselves account for the dynamic witnessed in sonnets 40–42 and elsewhere. Only the singular circumstances of a love relationship in which one person is disposed to inflict harm and the other is willing to accept the continuous pain caused by deliberate betrayal, only such circumstances can help explain some of the motives behind the pattern of tortuous actions and reactions that shape the continuing development of the sequence.

NINE

The Strength of Laws

Sonnets 43–74 contain prolonged meditations on a group of inter-related themes—all of which are by now familiar. After the crisis in sonnets 40–42, the relationship between the poet and the friend continues, but there are frequent references to separation, and a number of the poems are subdued—even melancholy—in response to the young man's most recent infidelity. Absence seems only to sharpen the poet's longing: "All days are nights to see till I see thee" (43); "I must attend time's leisure with my moan" (44); and in 45, the poet is assured (by the elements of air and fire) of his friend's "fair health," but,

> This told, I joy, but then no longer glad,
> I send them back again and straight grow sad.
>
> (45)

Despite their tone, these are sonnets of love and praise, and they continue as a leitmotif throughout 46, 47, 50 ("My grief lies onward and my joy behind"), 51, and 52:

> Blessed are you whose worthiness gives scope,
> Being had to triumph, being lacked, to hope.
>
> (52)

It is not surprising that the poet, in his determination to sustain the relationship, should continue to offer sonnets of praise—although they are now rarely lyrical or joyous—but it is unexpected that they should now alternate with an increasing number of poems in a very different key. In effect, the poet cannot entirely suppress his sense of reality—of the seriously damaged nature of the love relationship—and we find a growing number (and density) of sonnets that in various ways question or accuse the young man: 48, 49, 53, 57, 58, 61, 67–70. This line of development constitutes a form of quest on the part of the poet to probe, discover, and then to sharply criticize what he believes to be the real nature of the friend: Is he loving, or not? Is he capable of constancy, or not? A climax is reached in sonnets 69–70, where the youth is said to have the "rank smell of weeds" (69)—he has grown "common."

This attack is sharper than any previous one, but immediately afterward (in 71–74) the poet steps back, criticizing himself (as he has done before). Having pressed his case against the friend very far, he begins to denigrate both himself and his verse (which he declares to be "nothing worth"). Indeed, he wonders—as he had in sonnet 36—whether his very existence may dishonor the young man. He begins to focus on his own eventual death as a way of freeing the friend from any disrepute. He then (in sonnet 74) regains some confidence, defining his verse in positive terms that may—or may not—prove to be acceptable to the friend.

Sonnets 43–74 also include a number of poems on the subject of Time (54, 55, 59, 60, 63, 64, 65). In the first three, the poet is confident in believing that he can easily overcome Time's powers. In sonnet 60 he is less assured (hoping that his verse "shall stand"), and by 63–65 he is far from certain that he can overcome—or even withstand—the forces that Time has aligned against him. The accumulated shocks of past experience, and the poet's growing sense of mutability, have deeply shaken his confidence: beauty is seen to be far more vulnerable than before, preparing us for its declining importance as an absolute value in the final poems devoted to the friend (109–26).

The nuanced shifts in tone and meaning in sonnets 43–74 are difficult to summarize. Rather than sudden acts of infidelity (as in 33 or 40), we witness a developing situation in which the poet must respond to (and perforce accept) the youth's nearly continuous absence and roaming. In an increasing number of poems—49, 58, 59, 61, 65, 66, 69—the poet is more profoundly moved, more powerless, more continually on the defensive, and then more aggressive than ever before. And toward the end of this large group, a certain order emerges: in thirteen of the last fifteen sonnets, we find four of the great sonnets on Time and its overwhelming power; four that focus on the dubious nature of the friend; and five in which the poet dwells on his own eventual death (in such a way as to appeal for an expression of love from the young man).

•

The best way to begin a more detailed discussion of sonnets 43–74 is by focusing on the poet's attempt to discover the true nature of the friend. The reconciliation that follows 40–42 is soon qualified by the poet's strong expressions of increasing anxiety. In sonnet 48, he is "careful" to guard all his possessions—even "trifles"—but has not been able to do the same with the heart of the beloved:

> But thou, to whom my jewels trifles are,
> Most worthy comfort, now my greatest grief,
> Thou best of dearest, and mine only care,
> Art left the prey of every vulgar thief.
> Thee have I not locked up in any chest,
> Save where thou art not, though I feel thou art,
> Within the gentle closure of my breast,
> From whence at pleasure thou mayst come and part;
> > And even thence thou wilt be stol'n, I fear,
> > For truth proves thievish for a prize so dear.

(48)

If some earlier sonnets were blunt in their critique of the friend, this is more self-conscious in its deliberate and controlled delivery of one thrust after another, with the sharpest coming in the last five lines. The friend treats even the most precious jewels of the poet as "trifles," while also leaving himself open to being "stol'n" by any determined "vulgar" thief.

"Vulgar" suggests that the young man may be susceptible to the companionship of more common marauders than before, and it looks forward to the encroachments of the infectious companions and malevolent slanderers who surround the youth in sonnets 67–70. In addition, we learn of an assumed freedom that the friend now exercises (and the poet, of necessity, accepts): the liberty to come and go whenever he chooses, at his own pleasure. In this sense, the nature of the relationship between the two men has fundamentally changed. The poet must be prepared to stand by, entirely dependent on the young man's whims and desires. The liberty that appeared—earlier—to be only episodic has now become a critical presumption governing the relationship between the two main figures from this point forward.

If the poet worries (in sonnet 48) that the youth may be stolen, his greatest fear (expressed in the very next poem) is that the young man will actually abandon him. The poet—older, ill-featured, unconfident—imagines, in extraordinarily moving verse, an eventual moment of rejection:

> Against that time (if ever that time come)
> When I shall see thee frown on my defects,
> Whenas thy love hath cast his utmost sum,
> Called to that audit by advised respects;
> Against that time when thou shalt strangely pass,
> And scarcely greet me with that sun, thine eye,
> When love converted from the thing it was
> Shall reasons find of settled gravity:
> Against that time do I ensconce me here
> Within the knowledge of mine own desert,

And this my hand against myself uprear,
To guard the lawful reasons on thy part:
    To leave poor me thou hast the strength of laws,
    Since why to love I can allege no cause.

(49)

These lines suggest how dramatically the situation has changed since sonnets 33–36 and 40–42. We have simply to remember the tone and imagery of those earlier poems in order to see how much greater the poet's degree of fear and anxiety have become in the face of a potential complete repudiation by the friend. The need to prepare oneself against the repeated threat, "Against that time"; the way in which particular moments are piercingly imagined ("see thee frown on my defects"; "thou shalt strangely pass, / And scarcely greet me"); the pervasive dread of losing one's love, and the effort to find a way to avoid it—all of these factors combine to express depths of feeling that have not previously been sounded.

The poet has few defenses against "that time," although the sonnet itself is a rhetorical effort to deflect the possibility of abandonment by dramatizing the consequences of such an act. And once again, the poet offers to defend the friend's action, should it come to pass. Very significantly, there is the pathos ("To leave poor me") of the couplet, with its apparent self-pity combined with an intimation of strength and power: "Since why to love I can allege no cause." The reasons for the friend's possible desertion have been framed mainly in negative terms—of accounting ("cast," "sum," "audit") or well-considered advantages and disadvantages ("advised respects"). In the last quatrain, a legal metaphor is introduced, with a focus on the supposed lack of evidence and arguments that the poet can marshal in his own defense. It is precisely this lack of evidence, however, that the poet uses to his own advantage:

To leave poor me thou hast the strength of laws,
Since why to love I can allege no cause.

(49)

The friend has the law and all its "reasons" on his side, but the poet suggests that the resort to legal proceedings reveals a fundamental lack of understanding on the part of the friend. The poet can "allege no cause" to prove that the young man should love him, because love cannot be compelled. Rather, it is unconstrained feeling and commitment, and the poet makes this clear with a combination of mock-ignorance and mock-innocence.

Sonnets 57–58 continue—and deepen—the situation defined in 49 (and 48): the poet has strong poetic capabilities, but the friend has the full freedom to do as he pleases. He is now a "sovereign," and the poet accepts the role of "slave," "servant," or "vassal" throughout both sonnets:

> Being your slave, what should I do but tend
> Upon the hours and times of your desire?
> I have no precious time at all to spend,
> Nor services to do till you require.
> Nor dare I chide the world-without-end hour
> Whilst I (my sovereign) watch the clock for you,
> Nor think the bitterness of absence sour
> When you have bid your servant once adieu.
> Nor dare I question with my jealous thought
> Where you may be, or your affairs suppose,
> But like a sad slave stay and think of nought
> Save where you are how happy you make those.
>> So true a fool is love that in your will
>> (Though you do any thing) he thinks no ill.

(57)

This is an intensely moving poem and (together with sonnet 58) represents a moment of the poet's deepest humiliation—a searing, abject state. The absolute liberty asserted by the friend in sonnet 48 is now taken for granted. The poet, still transfixed by love, is seeking to find a stance or role for himself in this transformed situation. From one point of view, he is, by the force of sheer circum-stances, helpless—a "slave" who can only wait, "watch the clock," and refrain from questioning the youth. In this sense, sonnet 57 is a poem in which the poet's self-abasement and isolation seem nearly absolute.

At the same time, the poem is more subtle than at first it may appear. It is profoundly ironic and, through its rhetoric, attacks the hubris, vanity, and nonchalance of the young man who acts as a "sovereign" and casually inflicts pain upon the poet. In response, the poet asks—with obvious sarcasm—what could possibly matter to him, except to wait idly by, without bitterness or jealousy? In-deed, why should he have the right to question where the friend might be—or what he might be doing? The poem then closes with a couplet that manages to express some part of the poet's complex feelings: if it seems at first to be a complete capitulation, it is soon discovered to be something much more:

So true a fool is love that in your will
(Though you do any thing) he thinks no ill.

(57)

Love's willingness to tolerate all assaults—however great the neglect or injury—is at one level worthy of ridicule: indeed, love is a "fool." But folly turns out to be the real test of being "true" and devoted. When measured by the world's values, the poet's love is absurd because it is so entirely at the mercy of the youth. By other standards, however, the poet is superior in his commitment and determined fidelity. In sonnet 58, once again, with uncon-cealed irony, he accuses the friend of appealing to his legal "rights": "your charter is so strong / That you yourself may privilege your time" (58).

The poet's devotion to an unswerving love—regardless of the young man's conduct—allows him to redefine his stance and cast himself in yet another role—that of protector. This is precisely what happens soon after sonnet 58, in 61: here, the poet feels no need to propitiate the friend, or be a vassal waiting for commands, or define constant love as if it were a form of folly. Instead, he discovers a new perspective and tone, in which finely modulated irony, obvious traces of jealousy, and a surprising generosity of spirit come together:

> Is it thy will thy image should keep open
> My heavy eyelids to the weary night?
> Dost thou desire my slumbers should be broken,
> While shadows like to thee do mock my sight?
> Is it thy spirit that thou send'st from thee
> So far from home into my deeds to pry,
> To find out shames and idle hours in me,
> The scope and tenor of thy jealousy?
> O no, thy love, though much, is not so great;
> It is my love that keeps mine eye awake,
> Mine own true love that doth my rest defeat,
> To play the watchman ever for thy sake.
>> For thee watch I, whilst thou dost wake elsewhere,
>> From me far off, with others all too near.
>
> (61)

This move to a more reflective mode (and the shift away from immediate fears or feelings of self-abasement) places the poet in a position to consider, far better than before, some of the realities of his relationship with the young man. The idea that the friend's love may be so great that it would keep the poet awake is quickly dismissed. The friend may perhaps love the poet "much," but not so much as to be deeply preoccupied with him. Instead, it is the poet's "own true love" that keeps him from rest or sleep: love that springs partly from jealousy but that is also described as simply "true"—as constant and faithful.

The friend continues to be "far off" when he pleases. But this fact has—at least for the moment—been largely absorbed and accepted. Indeed, the poet has now taken up the post of "watchman," not in the sense of a curious and merely self-interested observer, but rather as a guardian or protector. His love keeps him awake, partly because of jealousy, but more out of a sense of concern for the other—"ever for thy sake." This expression of love goes beyond the desire for mutuality, or an overriding worry about "others" who are "all too near." Rather, it is a form of generosity in the face of scarcely requited affection. Earlier, in sonnet 57, the poet had obediently tended "Upon the hours and times" of the friend's desire, while—abject—he continued to "watch the clock" for him. Now he assumes a more controlling position, watching the young man's potential misdeeds with some bitterness but also with a form of philosophic realism, solicitude, and even protective care.

TEN

Your Substance

Nearly all of the sonnets between 43 and 74 that have so far probed the identity of the young man have done so obliquely. But in sonnet 53 there is an apparent effort to go further:

> What is your substance, whereof are you made,
> That millions of strange shadows on you tend?
> Since every one hath, every one, one shade,
> And you, but one, can every shadow lend.
> Describe Adonis, and the counterfeit
> Is poorly imitated after you;
> On Helen's cheek all art of beauty set,
> And you in Grecian tires are painted new;
> Speak of the spring and foison of the year,
> The one doth shadow of your beauty show,
> The other as your bounty doth appear,
> And you in every blessed shape we know.
>
> (53)

The friend is at first mysterious, ambiguous, multifarious. "Millions" of shadows—of different identities—"tend" on him. He appears to have no fixed nature, and we expect the opening question to be answered in the lines that immediately follow. Instead, we find a clear movement toward a poem of praise, where the young man is said to be more beautiful than the "shadows"—or "counterfeit" images—of Adonis and Helen, or the "spring and foison of the year": indeed, he appears in "every blessed shape." This development is not sustained, however, and the couplet introduces an unexpected shift in tone and meaning:

> In all external grace you have some part,
> But you like none, none you, for constant heart.

(53)

Are these lines intended as a compliment to the young man? Or does the first line of the couplet call such strong attention to the youth's "external grace," reminding us that the sonnet has so far focused primarily on his beauty while leaving other matters unattended? From this point of view, the pronounced emphasis on the friend's "constant heart" in the very last line seems particularly ironic: either the friend (through the poet's hyperbole) is obliquely accused of infidelity, or he is urged to become as faithful as the poet pronounces him to be. In short, sonnet 53 embodies more than one significant shift throughout its progress: from its initial questioning and its vision of the friend's multifariousness, to its praise of the young man's external grace or beauty, to an apparent undercutting of that praise by the final thrust in the last line. All of this is managed with considerable ease, and yet the sonnet embodies fundamental tensions inherent in the poet's role: he is partly an inquirer confronted by an unfathomable companion; partly a sonneteer of praise; and partly a critic of someone who acts and roams freely at will.

Other tensions become evident in sonnets 54 and 55. In 54, we find canker roses that appear to look genuine. They

> Hang on such thorns, and play as wantonly,
> When summer's breath their masked buds discloses;
> But for their virtue only is their show,

66

They live unwooed, and unrespected fade,
Die to themselves. Sweet roses do not so . . .

(54)

After this extended description, we are half-prepared for the canker roses to be associated with the friend. Instead, we find a sudden counterstatement in the couplet: the young man is described
as someone whose eventual loss of beauty will be preserved like
sweet "odours":

And so of you, beauteous and lovely youth,
When that shall vade, my verse distills your truth.

(54)

As in sonnet 53, the poet alters our perspective and expectations.
He concludes, in this case, with words of praise and a reversion to
his own power to perpetuate the youth's beauty and truth.

This invocation of the enduring nature of the poet's verse
leads directly to the next sonnet (55), where the poet insists that
neither death nor "all oblivious enmity" shall stand in the way of
the friend's "memory." The difficulty here lies not in any internal
changes in tone, but in the poem's sudden display of heightened
rhetoric—heroic but self-conscious and hyperbolic. It is as if the
poet, following the complexity of sonnets 53–54, felt the need to
reaffirm his commitment in unequivocal terms, making clear the
fact that neither his love, nor his role as the young man's chosen
writer, has in any way diminished.

We may choose, of course, to take this poem at face value—as
a straightforward celebration of the youth and an assertion of the
enduring power of the poet's verse. But in its context, the sonnet
seems to be another example of the poet's search to define himself
in relation to the friend: in addition to this "reassuring" stance in
55, he has been, at various moments, waiting upon "time's leisure"
with his "moan" (43–47); at still other moments, overcome with

anxiety and fear (48–49); then powerless and abject (57–58); and, finally, jealous but protective (61).

•

The remaining poems (between 43 and 75) that focus on the friend come toward the very end of the series. They, too, have their tensions and ambiguities, but they are, in addition, characterized by the fact that they now place the young man in the context of a decidedly public world of slanderers and critics. The most important point about these four poems (67–70) is that they disclose—as suggested earlier—a line of development that ends with an unusually strong indictment of the youth, although we are still a considerable distance from the powerful feelings expressed later in sonnets 94–96. Indeed, the poet seems at first (in sonnets 67–68) to present the young man as innocent: he is seen (in 67) as the victim of others who are evil but, by associating with the youth, achieve an "advantage," partly by imitating his beauty with "false painting." We learn that Nature itself must draw upon the young man's features in order to show true beauty: "O him she stores, to show what wealth she had / In days long since, before these last so bad."

This praise has already been qualified, however, in the very opening lines of sonnet 67, where the youth is said to live "with infection": with his presence, he "graces impiety." If his tainted companions have taken the initiative in choosing to seek out the friend, he has nevertheless willingly agreed to associate with them: "sin" in fact "laces" itself with his society, and there is no evidence to suggest that he resists. The poet's criticism, however, is muted and the sonnet ends on a celebratory note.

The contrast between the present time and a previous era of true beauty is continued in the next sonnet, 68. Here, there is no obvious criticism to offset the poet's praise: the young man is used by Nature to show the "false Art" of the current age in contrast to earlier times. But in this sonnet (and in 67), the poet praises only the youth's *beauty*—his appearance. Truth and fidelity are never mentioned. It is not surprising, therefore, that the poet shifts his ground in the very next poem to take account of more than simple "outward" show:

> Those parts of thee that the world's eye doth view
> Want nothing that the thought of hearts can mend;
> All tongues (the voice of souls) give thee that due,
> Utt'ring bare truth, even so as foes commend.
> Thy outward thus with outward praise is crowned . . .
>
> (69)

Beyond beauty, however, there are of course other values and, at this point, those who praise the young man's appearance ultimately measure him in quite different ways:

> They look into the beauty of thy mind,
> And that in guess they measure by thy deeds;
> Then, churls, their thoughts (although their eyes were
>   kind)
> To thy fair flower add the rank smell of weeds:
>   But why thy odour matcheth not thy show,
>   The soil is this, that thou dost common grow.
>
> (69)

These final lines come with unanticipated explicitness and power: the "churls" have been right in their judgment, and the poet, uncharacteristically, moves to a forceful conclusion. The young man is no longer distinctive: he has been tainted by any number of transgressions and associations, and has now grown "common." Indeed, he is said to have the rank smell of weeds—an accusation far more scathing than any other before this point in the sequence.

In addition, we are now presented with a much more detailed view of the young man's (and the poet's) world. We learned earlier that the poet was sometimes "in disgrace" with "men's eyes" (29), and we have had—throughout the sequence—indications of other ominous figures (such as poetic rivals). In sonnets such as 33–35, there were mysterious other figures who lured the youth away from the poet. In 57–58, there were still others with whom he freely spent his time. In 67, there were companions who had "laced" themselves with the poet's society; and we now hear (in 69) about many "tongues" and even "foes" who confound their praise of him.

In other words, however intimate in tone the Sonnets seem to be, the actions described in these poems—and the characters who dominate the scene—are embedded in a public world where commentary, judgment, opinions, enmities, and rivalries are ubiquitous. This world encroaches even further upon the youth (and poet) in sonnet 70: "That thou are blamed shall not be thy defect, / For slander's mark was ever yet the fair." Blame and slander are everywhere, although the poet adds, "So thou be good, slander doth but approve / Thy worth the greater." Clearly, the main issue is whether the young man is in fact "good," and by now there is more than enough evidence to show that the answer is far from self-evidently positive. In the second quatrain of sonnet 70, an assertion that the youth's "prime" years were "unstained" can only be read ironically, particularly in the light of sonnet 69 and the couplet of 70:

If some suspect of ill masked not thy show,
Then thou alone kingdoms of hearts shouldst owe.

(70)

A "suspicion" of ill deeds hovers over the youth's "show," or appearance, and the suspicion is obviously not unfounded. Nevertheless, the poet withholds much of his firepower at this point. He has already discovered and defined far more of the young man's "substance"—at a deeper level than he perceived or articulated in the first 42 sonnets—and he has in fact revealed the "rank" and "common" nature of the youth. At the same time, he clearly wishes to avoid a full break in the relationship: sonnet 70 may be an exercise in irony, but (unlike 69) it stops short of overt condemnation. Rather, it moves as close to a defense of the friend as, under the circumstances, one could expect.

•

The sonnets just discussed give increased emphasis to a theme that has been present in the sequence from the beginning (and will continue to the end): the dichotomy between outward "show" and inner reality. It is a distinctly Shakespearean theme, and an essentially tragic one. We will find no serious trace of it in any other sonnet sequence, or indeed in other lyric poetry of Shakespeare's era. There are, however, obvious analogies in Shakespeare's plays, beginning with some of the problem plays—certainly *Troilus*—and moving through to *Hamlet, Othello, Lear,* and others. The Sonnets stop far short of tragedy, but the work contains many of the circumstances that constitute tragic experience. This includes the incapacity of characters to penetrate reality—beyond the *appearance* of what they encounter—as well as their sudden realization, at other moments, that appearance and reality may be fatally different from each other:

> Yet eyes this cunning want to grace their art:
> They draw but what they see, know not the heart.
>
> (24)

> Lascivious grace, in whom all ill well shows,
> Kill me with spites; yet we must not be foes.
>
> (40)

> What is your substance, whereof are you made . . .
> > In all external grace you have some part,
> > But you like none, none you, for constant heart.
> >
> > (53)

But for their virtue only is their show,
They live unwooed, and unrespected fade . . .

(54)

Those parts of thee that the world's eye doth view
Want nothing that the thought of hearts can mend . . .
They look into the beauty of thy mind,
And that in guess they measure by thy deeds;
Then, churls, their thoughts (although their eyes
   were kind)
To thy fair flower add the rank smell of weeds:
      But why thy odour matcheth not thy show,
      The soil is this, that thou dost common grow.

(69)

If some suspect of ill masked not thy show . . .

(70)

Thus have I had thee as a dream doth flatter,
In sleep a king, but waking no such matter.

(87)

How like Eve's apple doth thy beauty grow,
If thy sweet virtue answer not thy show!

(93)

They that have pow'r to hurt, and will do none,
That do not do the thing they most do show . . .
      Lilies that fester smell far worse than weeds.

(94)

So are those errors that in thee are seen
To truths translated, and for true things deemed.

(96)

This list could easily be extended. In one sense, the passages are repetitive. From another point of view, the earlier examples consist largely of observations, questions, and ironic comments, while the later lines are much closer to actual indictments: "the rank smell of weeds"; "thou dost common grow"; "some suspect of ill"; "How like Eve's apple doth thy beauty grow"; "Lilies that fester smell far worse than weeds."

If passion and blindness are never pressed to the point of tragic devastation in the Sonnets, the poet does at moments observe and describe experiences that lie close to the essence of tragedy, and these are given expression in poems that constitute some of the most moving verse of the entire work:

> Tired with all these, for restful death I cry:
> As to behold desert a beggar born,
> And needy nothing trimmed in jollity,
> And purest faith unhappily forsworn,
> And gilded honour shamefully misplaced,
> And maiden virtue rudely strumpeted,
> And right perfection wrongfully disgraced,
> And strength by limping sway disabled,
> And art made tongue-tied by authority,
> And folly (doctor-like) controlling skill,
> And simple truth miscalled simplicity,
> And captive good attending captain ill.
> > Tired with all these, from these would I be gone,
> > Save that to die, I leave my love alone.
>
> (66)

> Th'expense of spirit in a waste of shame
> Is lust in action, and till action, lust
> Is perjured, murd'rous, bloody, full of blame,
> Savage, extreme, rude, cruel, not to trust;
> Enjoyed no sooner but despised straight,

Past reason hunted, and no sooner had,
Past reason hated as a swallowed bait
On purpose laid to make the taker mad:
Mad in pursuit and in possession so,
Had, having, and in quest to have, extreme;
A bliss in proof, and proved, a very woe,
Before, a joy proposed, behind, a dream.
    All this the world well knows yet none knows well
    To shun the heaven that leads men to this hell.

(129)

Both of these sonnets stand out in the sequence, not because they are unrelated to its major themes, but because they achieve a level of insight into aspects of human existence that go far to free them from the immediacy of any specific context. And in each of these sonnets, there is a depth of perception and expressed desire that drives the poet either toward oblivion and self-annihilation in the face of evil (66), or toward compulsive actions whose power is so great as to be irresistible (129). This wish to remove oneself from reality and—by contrast—the drive to pursue realities that are self-destructive constitute two main poles of the Sonnets. On the one hand, we see the poet withdrawing when "in disgrace with Fortune and men's eyes" (29), or when confronted by "vulgar scandal" (112) or by his own lack of self-worth (71); on the other hand, we see him drawn magnetically to love and passion either for the young man or, far more fatefully, for the mistress.

ELEVEN

Fearful Meditations

The later sonnets on Time (60, 63–65) are closely related to the poems on the friend's character (67–70) as well as those concerning the poet's anticipation of his own eventual death (71–74). As such, they reflect the change in tone—including the greater fears, anxieties, and increased sense of powerlessness—that characterizes so many of the sonnets following 42. Clearly, the poet's compounded experience to this point has consisted in large part of desertions on the part of the friend—progressive defections and betrayals when truth and fidelity initially had been expected. These events, as well as the effects created by the encroaching world of rumor and slander, have converged to make mutability, not constancy, an increasingly dominant force in the sequence.

In addition, the poet's growing awareness of the slippage of time is now greater than before, and it anticipates sonnets such as 102, 104, and 107, where the poet wonders whether the youth's beauty may have already been touched by the passage of years. While the issue is not yet explicitly raised, there is a growing sense that beauty alone may not be sufficient to command the absolute love and binding commitment of the poet. Other elements—as we see in sonnets 116, 117, and 123–25—may prove in the end to be much more significant.

As a result, sonnets 60 and 63–65 reveal a marked shift from earlier poems in which procreation or the poet's verse were put

forward—with considerable confidence—as strong defenses against
the threat of destruction and decay. Here, for example, are a few
passages from the opening of the sequence:

> Thou art thy mother's glass, and she in thee
> Calls back the lovely April of her prime;
> So thou through windows of thine age shalt see,
> Despite of wrinkles, this thy golden time.
>
> (3)

> Then the conceit of this inconstant stay
> Sets you most rich in youth before my sight,
> Where wasteful Time debateth with Decay
> To change your day of youth to sullied night;
> And all in war with Time for love of you,
> As he takes from you, I engraft you new.
>
> (15)

> But thy eternal summer shall not fade,
> Nor lose possession of that fair thou ow'st,
> Nor shall Death brag thou wand'rest in his shade,
> When in eternal lines to time thou grow'st.
>
> (18)

The tone varies in these and similar passages, but the range is not
great, and the poet's level of self-certainty is considerable. Only in
sonnet 19 is there any evidence of greater tension, but even that
poem ends on a positive note. Then, in sonnet 55, the poet asserts
that he is invincible: "marble," "gilded monuments," "stone," "statues," "masonry," and everything that can be destroyed by war will
perish sooner than the speaker's "pow'rful rhyme." The friend's
memory will shine in verse, not sullied by "sluttish time": he will
"pace forth" and his praise will endure till the very day of judgment.

But if the poet experiences a moment of (rather hyperbolic)

exaltation in sonnet 55, it is short-lived. By sonnet 60, the poetry has an altogether different cast—and sonnet 65 presents us with an interesting contrast to the "heroic" 55, demonstrating how much the balance of power has altered:

> Since brass, nor stone, nor earth, nor boundless sea,
> But sad mortality o'er-sways their power,
> How with this rage shall beauty hold a plea,
> Whose action is no stronger than a flower?
> O how shall summer's honey breath hold out
> Against the wrackful siege of batt'ring days,
> When rocks impregnable are not so stout,
> Nor gates of steel so strong, but Time decays?
> O fearful meditation: Where, alack,
> Shall Time's best jewel from Time's chest lie hid?
> Or what strong hand can hold his swift foot back?
> Or who his spoil of beauty can forbid?
>   O none, unless this miracle have might,
>   That in black ink my love may still shine bright.
>
>   (65)

Now Time (not the poet or his verse) is presented as the major power, and the emphasis is on Time's capacity to destroy "brass," "stone," "rocks impregnable," and "gates of steel." "Sad mortality" oversways everything. The "action" of beauty, trying to withstand the "rage" it faces, "is no stronger than a flower." The confidence and even ease with which the poet spoke in many earlier poems has now given way to a "fearful meditation" whose end remains very much in doubt. Although there is an assertion of the poet's power in the couplet, it is a conditional one: no force can conquer time "unless" a "miracle" takes place. The "black ink" of the poet's verse may possibly—far from certainly—enable this miracle to happen.

Each of these later poems on Time is masterful—beautiful as well as moving—and one of the elements that makes them impressive, even magisterial, is the way in which Shakespeare's imagination constantly enlarges the scope of all that is under Time's sway: so much so that Time becomes a metaphor for the entire process of change and mutability in human and natural affairs. Equally significant, the young man's beauty is no longer the only focus of concentration. It is clearly present in sonnet 60 and certainly 63; yet in sonnet 64, we find not simply the extraordinary magnitude of all that past ages (and nature itself) have suffered, but an ending in which the poet's confidence is even more diminished, and beauty is not mentioned:

When I have seen by Time's fell hand defaced
The rich proud cost of outworn buried age,
When sometime lofty towers I see down razed,
And brass eternal slave to mortal rage;
When I have seen the hungry ocean gain
Advantage on the kingdom of the shore,
And the firm soil win of the wat'ry main,
Increasing store with loss, and loss with store;
When I have seen such interchange of state,
Or state itself confounded to decay,
Ruin hath taught me thus to ruminate,
That Time will come and take my love away.
     This thought is as a death, which cannot choose
     But weep to have that which it fears to lose.

(64)

"Buried" ages and "lofty towers" are both "defaced" or "razed," and the sense of an unbreakable cycle of ceaseless destructive movement is captured in the central lines of the poem: the "hungry ocean" gains on the shore, only to have the shore then conquer some part of the "wat'ry main": "Increasing store with loss, and loss with store." By the end of sonnet 64, not only have buried ages been mentioned, but also kingdoms and states where there are perpetual interchanges. Just as the poet "meditated" in sonnet 65, here he "ruminates" and comes to believe that "Time will come and take my love"—not simply my love's beauty—"away."

This is not to suggest that beauty is unimportant in these poems. It is to say only that beauty is less sharply and uniquely the primary focus, and that its capacity to hold out against the "wrackful siege" of "batt'ring days" seems more precarious. When compared with the overwhelming magnitude of Time's all-embracing power to destroy, beauty now seems extraordinarily vulnerable—"no stronger than a flower"—and this shift in emphasis anticipates even greater changes to come.

•

The final poems (71–74) between sonnets 43 and 74 are unusually complex. Like the sonnets on Time, they are concerned with the inevitability of change leading to death—in this case, the poet's own death. In addition, they dwell (once more) on the poet's sense of his own inadequacy, including that of his verse. Having accused the friend so strongly in 69–70 ("thou dost common grow"), he steps back in order to take on—again—the role of the disgraced partner whose association with the young man will serve only to dishonor the youth. His insecurities come to the fore: he now gives strong expression to them, precisely in order to ward off what he most fears.

One of the distinctive aspects of these sonnets is their transparent rhetorical purpose. They are obviously intended to evoke sympathy from the friend and, in doing so, they often fall into a form of pleading that amounts to extreme self-despising:

No longer mourn for me when I am dead . . .
Nay, if you read this line, remember not
The hand that writ it, for I love you so,
That I in your sweet thoughts would be forgot,
If thinking on me then should make you woe.

(71)

O lest the world should task you to recite
What merit lived in me that you should love,
After my death (dear love) forget me quite,
For you in me can nothing worthy prove . . .
     For I am shamed by that which I bring forth,
     And so should you, to love things nothing worth.

(72)

The earth can have but earth, which is his due . . .
So then thou hast but lost the dregs of life,
The prey of worms, my body being dead . . .
Too base of thee to be remembered . . .

(74)

Clearly, the poet hopes to be reassured. He wants to be told that
he and his verse (that which he "brings forth") are valued—indeed
treasured. His recent attack on the young man has resulted not
only in a form of guilt, but also in an increase in anxiety. It is in this
context that 71–74 should be read, including the famous sonnet 73
("That time of year")—a marvelously sustained poem, lyrical and
beautiful in its varied effects:

That time of year thou mayst in me behold
When yellow leaves, or none, or few, do hang
Upon those boughs which shake against the cold,
Bare ruined choirs, where late the sweet birds sang.
In me thou seest the twilight of such day
As after sunset fadeth in the west,
Which by and by black night doth take away,
Death's second self that seals up all in rest.
In me thou seest the glowing of such fire
That on the ashes of his youth doth lie,
As the death-bed whereon it must expire,
Consumed with that which it was nourished by.

(73)

The poet's stance has now changed completely, and it is in most (not all) respects very different from sonnets 71–72. There is no self-abasement. The voice is restrained, controlled, and the poet appears to present himself as part of a natural process, leading to the restfulness of death.

Nevertheless, the rhetoric of sonnet 73 is clearly intended (like 71–72) to evoke sympathy for the poet, as well as for the purported decline in his poetic powers. He now "shakes" against the cold. "Bare ruined choirs" have taken the place of boughs "where late the sweet birds sang." And if the poet's youth continues to glow, it has been largely consumed by the very vitality that it once possessed. Indeed, insofar as the poet's love and verse have been devoted so completely to the friend, the young man should value them all the more, because they have been expended so entirely in his service. By the end of 73, the poet asks the friend not only for sympathy—as he moves into twilight and darkness—but also for requited love:

> This thou perceiv'st, which makes thy love more strong,
> To love that well which thou must leave ere long.
>
> (73)

The poet's "request" comes in the form of an assertion. But the assertion, in turn, is essentially a hope—no more than that.

Although the rhetorical intention of sonnet 73 resembles—in certain respects—that of 71–72, death has now been accepted with something approaching serenity, not primarily as an escape from the poet's self-despising or from the mockery of the "wise world" (71). This shift—as well as the entire tone of 73—prepares the way for sonnet 74, where the poet insists that death is inconsequential: it leaves only the "dregs of life, / The prey of worms." What now matters is the poet's "spirit," embodied in his verse and left as a memorial for the friend:

> When thou reviewest this, thou dost review
> The very part was consecrate to thee:

The earth can have but earth, which is his due;
My spirit is thine, the better part of me.

(74)

Here, the emphasis is on an offering—a gift of spirit expressed in a consciously plain style. All trace of the physical world is left behind. The spirit, formerly "contained" by the body, has been transmuted into verse, now given as a perpetual reminder of the poet.

The sonnet's couplet may at first seem monotonic, yet it is eloquent in its fine simplicity, omitting any hint of ornament or hyperbole in order to achieve a form of discourse that is nearly absolute in its determined minimalism. Referring first to his body ("that"), then to his spirit ("that"), and then to his verse ("this"), the poet concludes:

The worth of that is that which it contains,
And that is this, and this with thee remains.

(74)

•

Any attempt to offer a summary of sonnets 43–74 is bound to be incomplete. The poet's effort to understand the friend's "substance"—as well as to define his own role in the relationship—constitutes by far the greatest number of these sonnets, until they finally reach a point (in 69–70) that is more accusatory than in any other previous poem. The "inner order" of the sequence has continued to move, and here reaches a further stage in the progress of its "sentiments."

Meanwhile, the several sonnets on Time (60, 63–65) reveal a poet whose hope for constancy and mutuality in love has been shattered more than once, and who now sees the beauty of the young man threatened—far more seriously than before—by "Time's injurious hand" (63). There is no capitulation to Time by the poet, but there is a far greater awareness of the extraordinary force with which he must contend, and the special power that may be required to overcome his adversary.

Finally, sonnets 71–74 focus on the poet's contemplated death, and on the worth of his poetry. This subject reinforces that of sonnet 66 and those on Time. Visions of the poet as "compounded . . . with clay" are a natural sequel to the "sad mortality" and "decay" of sonnet 65, although 71–74 are more than personal meditations. They are intended to evoke pity and elicit love on the part of the young man, and are yet another indication of the poet's fear of being cast aside—partly because of his shameful self, and partly because his verse may be viewed as "nothing worth." Sonnets 71–72 are particularly important, because they dwell on the poet's lack of "merit" and value—another retreat after the assertive attacks on the young man in 69–70.

Sonnets 73 and 74, however, represent an attempt by the poet to transform his own role and that of his poetry, which by 74 is defined as an offering. It is of course far from certain that this gift—in such a plain and minimalist style—will be sufficient to satisfy the friend, whose appetite for variety (whether in companionship, love, or poetry) is obviously considerable. Is the manner of sonnet 74 (or 71–73) as lively, "modern," and flattering as the young man may desire? The answer is obviously unclear, but this lack of clarity is soon resolved in a way that leads to yet another crisis in the sequence.

TWELVE

His Great Verse

The last few poems in the group of sonnets just discussed (43–74) form a transition to the set usually referred to as the rival poet series. The poet's concern in 71–74 about the value of his verse led him to deep expressions of doubt, as well to a positive affirmation. Meanwhile, sonnets 76–86 are poems that explicitly focus on the subject of poetic style and truth. They center on the friend's emerging desire to seek out other writers—and, eventually, a single writer— who can provide him with poetry characterized by the "fresher stamp" and "modern" manner that appear to be lacking in his own chosen poet. One major thrust of this series, therefore, is the development of a contest between the poet and a rival who will soon become—if only briefly—the favorite of the young man.

Beyond the level of incident, this group of sonnets has far-reaching consequences for the very concept of a poetry of praise. Several issues are at stake: the differences between praise and flattery; the possibility of creating a genuine poetry of praise when pervasive flattery threatens its very existence; the susceptibility and inconstancy of the friend, who enjoys being courted by new writers; and, finally, the change in the poet's own verse, which he has so often disparaged but which he now begins to use in new ways.

Although this set of sonnets seems to focus on a competition between different poets and their styles, that is ultimately not the fundamental issue. The most important question concerns the

friend's susceptibility to flattery and the extent of his commitment
or fidelity to the poet. That is to say, the young man is tested
and, once again, he defects. In this instance, his action is felt all
the more sharply because it comes with such deliberation, as if he
were enjoying the contest. In the end, it is the youth's vanity and
conceit that lead to his decision, despite the poet's continuing efforts
to warn him.

These sonnets are also performances by the poet, and their
rhetoric frequently takes the form of special (and certainly self-
interested) pleading. He characterizes the rival's verse as fashionable
(and "false") art and ornament, casting himself as a plain-speaking,
truth-telling "unlettered clerk" whose only goal is to portray the
friend quite simply as he is:

> But he that writes of you, if he can tell
> That you are you, so dignifies his story.
> Let him but copy what in you is writ,
> Not making worse what nature made so clear . . .
>
> (84)

In view of the poet's desire to avoid all forms of overt flattery
and artifice, his only stylistic alternatives are to repeat, in a variety
of ways, what he has already said ("That you are you"), or else to
lapse into silence, widening the gulf between himself and the
young man (who now craves habitual praise):

> This silence for my sin you did impute,
> Which shall be most my glory, being dumb;
> For I impair not beauty, being mute,
> When others would give life, and bring a tomb.
>
> (83)

If silence and plainness seem to be the poet's main available
defenses, he must nevertheless find new ways to make use of

them—again and again, in sonnet after sonnet. Here, his capacity for impressive rhetorical performance and dramatic responsiveness is self-evident:

> Why is my verse so barren of new pride?
> So far from variation or quick change?
>
> (76)

> O how I faint when I of you do write,
> Knowing a better spirit doth use your name . . .
>
> (80)

> I grant thou wert not married to my Muse . . .
>
> (82)

> Was it the proud full sail of his great verse,
> Bound for the prize of (all too precious) you . . . ?
>
> (86)

It is clear, even from scattered lines such as these, that the poet uses all his rhetorical weaponry in this set of sonnets, especially at those moments when he seems most at bay. In one poem after another, the speaker warns the friend not to give ear to "every alien pen." While the young man may not have been lawfully married to the poet's muse (and he therefore has the supposed right to peruse and accept all the flattering "dedicated words" written to him), he is—from the poet's perspective—breaking his vows, and he succumbs fully to his own inflated sense of self. In short, the poet offers a critique of both the youth and the rival: he articulates the moral values at stake and defines his own role as someone who praises—and expresses his love for—the friend, attempting only to copy what nature has bestowed upon the young man.

Sonnet 80 alludes to several of these matters, and by the end of the poem, we have come to see why the friend, not the rival, is the key protagonist in the combat under way:

> O how I faint when I of you do write,
> Knowing a better spirit doth use your name,
> And in the praise thereof spends all his might,
> To make me tongue-tied speaking of your fame.
> But since your worth (wide as the ocean is)
> The humble as the proudest sail doth bear,
> My saucy bark (inferior far to his)
> On your broad main doth wilfully appear.
> Your shallowest help will hold me up afloat,
> Whilst he upon your soundless deep doth ride,
> Or (being wracked) I am a worthless boat,
> He of tall building and of goodly pride.
> > Then if he thrive and I be cast away,
> > The worst was this: my love was my decay.

(80)

Questions concerning the tone of this poem are raised, even in the first four lines. Is the opening of the sonnet an expression of actual anxieties on the part of the poet ("O how I faint") or an ironic way of dismissing the rival? We may be initially uncertain, but by the end of the poem, it is clear that irony has prevailed. The rival (it is said) must spend *all* "his might" in an effort to make the poet "tongue-tied," and in the next quatrain we are offered the first hint of the rival's greatest fault—his unabashed pride and self-conscious impressiveness (he is the "proudest sail"). The poet (in 76) had asked—with mock-innocence—why his own verse was "so barren" of "pride" or pretention. Now we are told that the rival's overriding characteristic is his "goodly pride." In other words, the self-important character of the rival parallels the nature of his hyperbolic verse, and these qualities are highlighted in the last poem of this group (86), where "the proud full sail of his great verse" is invoked. The poet's real challenge, therefore, is to persuade the friend that he has no need of "proud full" fashionable sonnets to make him seem even more fair than is already the case.

In the second quatrain of sonnet 80, the friend's worth (his fidelity and steadfastness) is said to be as "wide as the ocean," but given his previous betrayals (and the poet's apprehensions about him), there is every reason to doubt whether that worth will be sufficient. In fact, when the poet characterizes himself as "saucy"—and his sudden appearance as "willful"—he is by then challenging the young man as much as the rival. He looks directly, first and foremost, to the youth for a sign of approval and for aid: "Your shallowest help will hold me up afloat." Everything depends on the friend, including his capacity to understand what is at stake, and to make the right choice.

No answer is forthcoming in sonnet 80, but the couplet contains an intimation of what may eventually occur:

> Then if he thrive and I be cast away,
> The worst was this: my love was my decay.
>
> (80)

Here, in the face of a possible defeat and defection, the poet continues to assert that his own feelings of love and faithfulness would be "the worst" that could be said of him, if he were to be cast aside. In this sense, the couplet of 80 is in some ways similar to that of 49: there is pathos, and an element of self-pity (and pleading), in all of these lines. But, as suggested earlier, there is also a note of triumph. The poet presents himself as the openhearted partner who may soon endure repudiation, while he continues to love without resort to "argument":

> To leave poor me thou hast the strength of laws,
> Since why to love I can allege no cause.
>
> (49)

•

During the course of the rival poet series, the tension is steadily increased and the poet heightens his criticism of the young man, striking at his vanity, until the climax is reached in sonnet 86. He does not simply argue his case, but makes his point more emphatically by adopting a style of deliberate plain-speaking (82 and 85) as well as by withdrawing into silence (83, 85, 86). An implicit continuous dialogue takes place between him and the young man, especially in sonnets such as 82, where the poet responds to the youth's assertion that he is free to do as he pleases. The poet concedes the fact, but does so in a way that makes the young man's transgression and vanity clear:

> I grant thou wert not married to my Muse,
> And therefore mayst without attaint o'erlook
> The dedicated words which writers use
> Of their fair subject, blessing every book.
> Thou art as fair in knowledge as in hue,
> Finding thy worth a limit past my praise,
> And therefore art enforced to seek anew
> Some fresher stamp of the time-bettering days.

(82)

Ever since the marriage poems at the beginning of the sequence, the poet's presumption has been (in spite of all the lapses) that he and the friend have continued to be metaphorically married, not only through love but also through the poet's role as chosen writer. Now both bonds are in the process of being broken: the young man relishes the many words and books dedicated to him. No threat of "attaint" can bind him, having concluded that his own worth is so great that it exceeds the poet's ability to adequately praise him. He is "enforced" to seek a new poet and "fresher" verse to suit the mode of "time-bettering days." The ironies here are multiple, scarcely needing explication. Perhaps the deepest of all resides in the fact that, rather than seeking something (such as the poet's own verse) that might withstand the ravages of Time, the young man embraces mutability—all that is new and changing, just as fashions change. Then, in sonnet 84, near the conclusion of this group, the poet undertakes a direct assault. He begins with a familiar rationale: "But he that writes of you, if he can tell / That you are you, so dignifies his story." Yet this is evidently not enough for the youth, and the poet concludes in the couplet that

> You to your beauteous blessings add a curse,
> Being fond on praise, which makes your praises worse.
>
> (84)

•

Following the friend's decision to seek poetry that is newly minted, the poet withdraws, distancing himself from the hyperbolic verse that current "modern quills" produce. In a sea of flattery, the poet proceeds to show what he alone can bring:

> I think good thoughts, whilst others write good words,
> And like unlettered clerk still cry "Amen" . . .
> Hearing you praised, I say, " 'Tis so, 'tis true,"
> And to the most of praise add something more;
> But that is in my thought, whose love to you
> (Though words come hindmost) holds his rank before.
>   Then others for the breath of words respect,
>   Me for my dumb thoughts, speaking in effect.
>
> (85)

In a sonnet that echoes aspects of 23, the poet offers only the briefest and simplest of utterances. The wit of the opening lines soon gives way to something more serious. The poet, uniquely, brings his "love to you," and this outweighs all words of praise—indeed any words at all. "Dumb thoughts" are sufficient, and they make clear that it is not simply the silence that matters, but the love that is expressed by means of the silence.

Sonnet 86 marks the culmination of this group, and is one of the great poems of the sequence. Here, the poet seems at first to acknowledge that he has been "sick" with "fear" and that his verse was "inhearsed" by the power of the rival's poetry:

> Was it the proud full sail of his great verse,
> Bound for the prize of (all too precious) you,
> That did my ripe thoughts in my brain inhearse,
> Making their tomb the womb wherein they grew?
> Was it his spirit, by spirits taught to write
> Above a mortal pitch, that struck me dead?
> No, neither he, nor his compeers by night
> Giving him aid, my verse astonished.
> He, nor that affable familiar ghost
> Which nightly gulls him with intelligence,
> As victors of my silence cannot boast . . .
>
> (86)

The opening lines are energized by questions that expose the rapacious motives of the "proud full" rival, and characterize the friend as a "prize" who is "all too precious." Sarcasm, as well as conscious hyperbole ("Above a mortal pitch") set the tone, and it quickly becomes clear that the initial questions are in fact purely rhetorical: their effectiveness ultimately depends on the fact that they are indirect but powerful criticisms of the young man. "Struck me dead" comes with special force, placed as it is at the end of the second (and last) question—which is then followed by an emphatic "No" (and then by the description of a conspiratorial nighttime scene). Although there are considerable forces aligned against the poet, the "compeers" are treated lightly and even amusingly: the "affable familiar ghost" is brushed off with a dash of wit, and the word *gulls* puts the nature of the "intelligence" very nicely in its place. In short, the poetic power of the rival poet is greatly diminished: he cannot compose verse on his own, but must rely on the aid of others (which proves to be ineffective). The weight of the final lines, with their restrained gravity, falls entirely on the friend:

> I was not sick of any fear from thence.
>> But when your countenance filled up his line,
>> Then lacked I matter, that enfeebled mine.

(86)

The poet's concern has had nothing to do with the supposed superiority of the rival's verse. Instead, his "fear" was that the rival would seek—through flattery and his poetry's "fresher stamp"—to capture and win possession of the friend. Even more devastating was the fear that the young man would accept the rival's offerings, and perhaps even return his friendship. For the moment, the desertion takes place, and the friend's countenance "fills" the lines of the rival's verse, "astonishing" the poet. With his friend momentarily gone, the poet inevitably lacks "matter"—lacks a subject, indeed his only subject. He is now compelled to be silent—not by choice, but because, for the time being, he no longer has anything or anyone to write about.

•

The rival poet sonnets present us with several important insights. The poet is temporarily abandoned, and the experience is more profound than any previous one in the sequence, because it follows a prolonged combat in which repudiation comes only after much delay, with the friend's full knowledge that the poet's love—not simply his poetry—is at stake. All of the poet's powers and strategies have, over an extended period of time, been employed and exhausted—but to no avail.

Moreover, the friend's desertion is yet one more act not only of infidelity, but of dispossession. It is also a form of usurpation, analogous to the earlier usurpation of the poet's mistress by the friend. The poet's "seat" has once again been taken by another. He has been further stripped of his dwindling "possessions." This conception of repeated loss, and the need to absorb and adapt to it, continues as a major subject of the sequence and will recur once more in the last section of the work. At the same time, it soon becomes clear that this most recent betrayal by the friend is not final. As in all other instances of apparent abandonment, the relationship survives and leads to a series of love poems that take us much further than anything we have witnessed before.

THIRTEEN

O, *What a Mansion*

The sonnets that immediately follow the rival poet series fall into two distinct but related groups. The first (87–93) reveals a familiar pattern: the young man appears to have abandoned the poet, who responds with a sonnet of strong protest (87). Then, in a swift reversal, the poet once again adopts the role of willing scapegoat, declaring himself unworthy and taking upon himself the blame for all misdeeds (88–90). The presumption in these poems is that the poet and the young man are bound in a curious but still unbroken relationship with each other, and that they achieve a tentative but fragile reconciliation—something that becomes even clearer in sonnets 91–93, when the poet seems to resign himself to perpetual uncertainty: "So shall I live, supposing thou art true" (93).

This state of mind proves, however, to be intolerable. In the second related group of sonnets (94–96), the poet once more takes the offensive and pursues his effort to characterize the young man, unmasking all his faults with greater precision, force, and even ferocity than ever before. By sonnets 95–96, the poet's condemnation is so unequivocal that it leads to a prolonged separation, to be followed much later by another reunion.

•

Since the poet has already experienced several betrayals and reconciliations, it is not surprising that we should now—following the young man's choice of the rival—hear a voice that is (in sonnet 87) controlled and even audacious, in sharp contrast to that of earlier examples:

> Farewell, thou art too dear for my possessing,
> And like enough thou know'st thy estimate;
> The charter of thy worth gives thee releasing:
> My bonds in thee are all determinate.
> For how do I hold thee but by thy granting?
> And for that riches where is my deserving?
> The cause of this fair gift in me is wanting,
> And so my patent back again is swerving.
> Thy self thou gav'st, thy own worth then not knowing,
> Or me, to whom thou gav'st it, else mistaking;
> So thy great gift, upon misprision growing,
> Comes home again, on better judgement making.
> > Thus have I had thee as a dream doth flatter,
> > In sleep a king, but waking no such matter.

(87)

The poet has taken the initiative—it is *his* "Farewell" and the friend is in his "possession." The cause of the break is attributed to the friend's purported increase in value: he has become "too dear" and the poet can, in effect, no longer afford him. There is obviously a great deal of irony in these lines: the friend "like enough" knows his own (exaggerated) worth. Indeed, he has already been described in sonnet 86 as a "prize"—as "(all too precious) you." Earlier he had enjoyed the "dedicated words" addressed to him by other writers and had become too "fond on praise." Now, in 87, his "riches" have become so great that the poet can no longer satisfy the young man's claims.

The poet's effort to reassert control of the situation is essentially rhetorical. He realizes only too well that he lacks the power to alter the course of events: "For how do I hold thee but by thy granting?" Nevertheless, his tone is scarcely compliant—associating the friend once again with images and metaphors derived from the realm of law and finance: "estimate," "charter," "bonds," "granting," "patent," and the punning on "worth." These prudential terms and their worldly connotations are in sharp contrast to the poet's, which are focused on the gift of freely given love:

> Thy self thou gav'st, thy own worth then not knowing,
> Or me, to whom thou gav'st it, else mistaking . . .

(87)

Finally, the closing couplet combines restrained bitterness with something approaching a quietly forceful statement of fact, fully within the poet's emotional control:

> Thus have I had thee as a dream doth flatter,
> In sleep a king, but waking no such matter.

(87)

The last phrase ("no such matter") is a consciously colloquial understatement. There is no dramatic expression of dismay, because the poet is far beyond the comparative innocence and susceptibility to shock that he had registered in response to earlier betrayals.

In its entirety, sonnet 87 is as much a bid to sustain the relationship with the young man as it is an expression of "farewell." The rhetoric of the poem is intended to force the friend to confront the implications of his most recent desertion. The young man has been defined as transparently vain and self-important; he must have been "mistaken" when he calculated the "worth" of the poet (and himself); he has acted according to the cool dictates of "better judgement" instead of giving any part of himself to the poet. In short, the sonnet drives home a persistent critique of the youth, with familiar charges (as well as some new ones). The hope is that the friend will not leave definitively, and this proves indeed to be the case.

Interestingly, the poet—with undisguised irony—suggests in

sonnet 87 that he may be an unworthy partner ("where is my deserving?") who has no right to the friend's "fair gift" (the cause is "wanting"). Then, suddenly, the irony vanishes and in the very next poem (88) the poet shifts his ground, declaring himself to be "weak" and shameful. In other words, he blames himself and begins to submit as he had in sonnets 36 and 71–72, although his tone is now under firm control and there is none of the deep self-abasement revealed earlier. When the poet professes to take all disgrace upon himself, he does so with no show of turbulent feeling or evident internal struggle. Having experienced several transgressions, the role of the tainted partner is now assumed with some obvious irony but also with comparative equanimity:

> When thou shalt be disposed to set me light,
> And place my merit in the eye of scorn,
> Upon thy side against myself I'll fight,
> And prove thee virtuous, though thou art forsworn:
> With mine own weakness being best acquainted,
> Upon thy part I can set down a story
> Of faults concealed wherein I am attainted,
> That thou in losing me shall win much glory;
> And I by this will be a gainer too,
> For, bending all my loving thoughts on thee,
> The injuries that to myself I do,
> Doing thee vantage, double vantage me.
>> Such is my love, to thee I so belong,
>> That for thy right myself will bear all wrong.

(88)

In addition to the relative ease with which the poet accepts the friend's transgression, he expresses a willingness to fight against himself in order to "prove thee virtuous." In fact, he offers to tell a story of his own hidden faults in a way that is almost casual. In the final lines, he makes clear, once again, that his own deep feelings ("Such is my love") are the only reason for his compliance.

In the next sonnet, the poet continues to play the role of the dishonored one who deserves whatever accusations the friend may choose to make, but the tone changes in important ways:

> Say that thou didst forsake me for some fault,
> And I will comment upon that offence;
> Speak of my lameness, and I straight will halt,
> Against thy reasons making no defence.
> Thou canst not (love) disgrace me half so ill,
> To set a form upon desired change,
> As I'll myself disgrace; knowing thy will,
> I will acquaintance strangle and look strange,
> Be absent from thy walks, and in my tongue
> Thy sweet beloved name no more shall dwell,
> Lest I (too much profane) should do it wrong,
> And haply of our old acquaintance tell.
> > For thee, against myself I'll vow debate,
> > For I must ne'er love him whom thou dost hate.
>
> (89)

Throughout the Sonnets, the poet's love is often expressed in terms of apprehension, fear of loss, shock at the discovery of infidelity, or the humiliation and the servility of "vassalage." We are rarely given any sense of the intimacy of the love relationship: very little that makes it alive and helps to dramatize its meaning to the poet. In sonnet 49, we were offered glimpses, even though the fear of loss was dominant:

> Against that time (if ever that time come)
> When I shall see thee frown on my defects . . .
> Against that time when thou shalt strangely pass,
> And scarcely greet me with that sun, thine eye . . .
>
> (49)

Here, we can feel the closeness between the two men, simply

through the mode of direct address ("thee," "thou," "thine"), and the desire for a familiar greeting that never materializes. Sonnet 89 goes much further, creating vignettes of what the love has meant in the past—its tenderness ("Thou canst not (love)"); its companionable intimacy in remembered walks and conversations; and its survival through time—the relationship now described as "our old acquaintance." It will be the poet (not the friend) who will—for the sake of love—pass and "look strange," in his torturous effort to cease all contact, not suddenly, but through the effort to "strangle" it. It is against this backdrop that the poet's moments of self-abasement and his dependence on the young man must be judged, in order to comprehend the power of the poet's emotions and his apparent determination to do whatever is necessary to sustain the relationship.

Sonnet 89 ends with the suggestion that the friend might come to "hate" him. As the last word in the poem, *hate* carries unusual weight, intensifying the feelings at stake, though neither the word nor the emotion is new to the sequence: in sonnet 10, the young man was seen to be "possessed with murd'rous hate," and in 40, the poet spoke of "hate's known injury." In sonnet 90, one of the most moving sonnets of the sequence, the poet anticipates—while trying to ward off—the hatred that might indeed come:

> Then hate me when thou wilt, if ever, now,
> Now while the world is bent my deeds to cross,
> Join with the spite of Fortune, make me bow,
> And do not drop in for an after-loss.
> Ah do not, when my heart hath scaped this sorrow,
> Come in the rearward of a conquered woe;
> Give not a windy night a rainy morrow,
> To linger out a purposed overthrow.
> If thou wilt leave me, do not leave me last,
> When other petty griefs have done their spite,
> But in the onset come; so shall I taste

At first the very worst of Fortune's might;
    And other strains of woe, which now seem woe,
    Compared with loss of thee, will not seem so.

(90)

Each line and quatrain builds with greater intensity on the preceding one, and the striking sound effects of stressed words and syllables sustain an air of controlled crisis: even in the first two or three lines we feel the effect of the strong monosyllables: *hate, wilt, now, bent, spite, make, bow.* And at the end, we find not only monosyllables: *wilt, last, petty, spite, onset, taste, first, worst, Fortune's, might.* The intent is to persuade the friend neither to hate nor to leave the poet. The focus is now on the young man's potential for cruelty ("do not drop in for an after-loss") or on his capacity to inflict pain as if sadistically: do not "linger out a purposed overthrow."

In the very next sonnet (91), the poet imagines not another scene of parting, but one that expresses his continued feelings of love, while also stressing the fragility of the relationship between the two men: "thou mayst take / All this away, and me most wretched make." Then, in sonnet 92, he repeats his devotion to the young man, and indicates—again—that a tentative reunion has taken place (while also acknowledging his deep bewilderment): "Thou mayst be false, and yet I know it not." This leads (in 93) to a poignant expression of the poet's increasingly intolerable predicament:

So shall I live, supposing thou art true,
Like a deceived husband; so love's face
May still seem love to me, though altered new . . .

(93)

As sonnet 93 proceeds, the poet dwells increasingly on the young man's impenetrability and his capacity for deception:

In many's looks, the false heart's history
Is writ in moods and frowns and wrinkles strange,
But heaven in thy creation did decree
That in thy face sweet love should ever dwell;
Whate'er thy thoughts or thy heart's workings be,
Thy looks should nothing thence but sweetness tell.
How like Eve's apple doth thy beauty grow,
If thy sweet virtue answer not thy show!

(93)

By the end of this sonnet, the poet has stressed the potential discrepancy between what one *shows* and what one may actually *be*. "How like Eve's apple" strikes one first as a characterization of the friend, and represents a further step in the poet's steady "discovery" of the young man's nature—although the statement is of course immediately qualified by the sonnet's last line. Following this development, three related sonnets (94–96) then introduce the strongest indictment of the young man in the entire sequence. The first (94) strikes a different note: it opens with allusions to the friend's coldness—his apparent self-sufficiency and restraint—which appears to prevent him from giving in to common temptations. If so, the friend is entitled to "heaven's graces": he is rightly the "lord" and "owner" of his "face."

They that have pow'r to hurt, and will do none,
That do not do the thing they most do show,
Who, moving others, are themselves as stone,
Unmoved, cold, and to temptation slow—
They rightly do inherit heaven's graces,
And husband nature's riches from expense;
They are the lords and owners of their faces,
Others but stewards of their excellence.
The summer's flow'r is to the summer sweet,
Though to itself it only live and die,

But if that flow'r with base infection meet,
The basest weed outbraves his dignity:
> For sweetest things turn sourest by their deeds;
> Lilies that fester smell far worse than weeds.

(94)

The language of the poem is clearly double-edged. The description of the young man recalls his characterization in the marriage sonnets: unresponsive, self-centered, living only for himself, "owning" himself rather than being a good steward of what nature has only loaned—not given—to him. To be "cold," therefore, is in most respects not admirable, though it may help to protect one from temptation.

By this point, however, the poet has already begun to suggest multiple interpretations of the friend. He may perhaps be cold and virtuous, and he may appear to resist temptation, but ultimately may not do so—in which case, he embodies hypocrisy as well as inconstancy. Finally, he may simply be unfathomable: beauteous in show but unpredictable in action, and therefore capable of both commitment and infidelity. Given these alternatives, the poet chooses to warn rather than explicitly condemn the friend:

But if that flow'r with base infection meet,
The basest weed outbraves his dignity:
> For sweetest things turn sourest by their deeds;
> Lilies that fester smell far worse than weeds.

(94)

Warnings are a convenient way of sidestepping direct accusations, although in this case, the force of the gesture is tantamount to an accusation. The "if" in line 11 is just barely conditional. The clear implication is that "infection" is all but certain, and that the "lilies" may indeed be festering.

Sonnets 95 and 96 bring to a conclusion the large number of

poems that have dwelt on the friend's nature. They draw on the language of several previous sonnets, but press well beyond them. For example, in sonnet 54, the contrast between "canker" and "perfumed" roses was fully exploited, but the poem ended with the suggestion that the "beauteous and lovely youth" was a genuine rose that would survive in the poet's verse. A somewhat different but similar comparison (and conclusion) marked sonnet 70, where "canker vice" was said to prey upon "the sweetest buds," but there again the youth was—with considerable irony—said to be free of any such danger, in spite of the slanderous and envious voices that surrounded him. By sonnet 95, however, the change is abundantly clear:

> How sweet and lovely dost thou make the shame
> Which, like a canker in the fragrant rose,
> Doth spot the beauty of thy budding name!
> O, in what sweets dost thou thy sins enclose!
> That tongue that tells the story of thy days
> (Making lascivious comments on thy sport)
> Cannot dispraise but in a kind of praise,
> Naming thy name blesses an ill report.
> O, what a mansion have those vices got
> Which for their habitation chose out thee,
> Where beauty's veil doth cover every blot,
> And all things turns to fair that eyes can see!
> >   Take heed (dear heart) of this large privilege:
> >   The hardest knife ill-used doth lose his edge.

(95)

The poet's attack could scarcely be more direct than in these lines, although the final couplet seems to soften the assault with a warning ("Take heed (dear heart)")—an effort to sustain some trace of the love relationship while (in the rest of the sonnet) undermining its very foundations. The young man has brought shame upon his name (by "spotting" or staining it); he is guilty of sins, of lascivious sport, and of vices. Yet his appearance—his "privilege" or power—is such that all faults are effectively veiled by his sheer beauty. He converts evil into an appearance of good, covers "every blot," and "turns to fair" everything "that eyes can see." By this time, all doubts about his true nature have vanished:

> O what a mansion have those vices got
> Which for their habitation chose out thee . . .
>
> (95)

Throughout the sequence, the young man has frequently been defined in contradictory or oxymoronic terms: a "sweet thief" or "tender churl" who prompted the poet to ask (in sonnet 10), "Shall hate be fairer lodged than gentle love?" Now self-contradiction—which has become a form of deception—is seen to be at his very core: he makes "shame" into something "sweet and lovely"; he encloses his "sins" in "sweets"; and even if one "dispraises" him, the very words cannot help but turn into "a kind of praise." He becomes a beauteous habitation for vice.

Having come thus far, the question is whether the poet should cease his attack—if only to salvage some part of the relationship—or whether he should press further. Perhaps surprisingly, he chooses the latter course, although in the last lines of the next sonnet, he resorts to an approach that is more conditional:

> Some say thy fault is youth, some wantonness,
> Some say thy grace is youth and gentle sport;
> Both grace and faults are loved of more and less:
> Thou mak'st faults graces that to thee resort.
> As on the finger of a throned queen
> The basest jewel will be well esteemed,
> So are those errors that in thee are seen
> To truths translated, and for true things deemed.

How many lambs might the stern wolf betray,
If like a lamb he could his looks translate!
How many gazers mightst thou lead away,
If thou wouldst use the strength of all thy state!
    But do not so; I love thee in such sort,
    As thou being mine, mine is thy good report.

(96)

Sonnet 96 is more tempered than 95, and there is at first some artful distancing—"Some say . . . Some say." Nevertheless, the poet takes the direct lead in lines 5–8, when the friend is said to be "base" like the false jewel of a "throned queen," transforming "errors" into apparent truth. Moreover, the poet includes himself, by implication, among those who have been susceptible to the youth: "How many gazers mightst thou lead away, / If thou wouldst use the strength of all thy state!" Throughout the sequence, much of that "strength" has been "used"; and even now the poet allows himself to be "led away" once more, in the surprising—and almost certainly misplaced—couplet (repeated from sonnet 36): "I love thee in such sort, / As thou being mine, mine is thy good report."

By the end of sonnet 96, the friend seems to be finally known and revealed for what he is. But there is, as one might expect, nothing definitive about this apparent conclusion. He has now been condemned much more directly and powerfully than in any previous sonnet, bringing this line of development to a finale. But this does not necessarily end the relationship between the poet and the young man. It does not eliminate the youth's magnetism, grace, beauty, and charm. In fact, he will—somewhat later—reveal himself to be strongly affected by a sudden act of betrayal on the part of the poet.

FOURTEEN

This Most Balmy Time

Following the poet's sustained and fierce assault on the friend's integrity in sonnets 95–96, a prolonged separation takes place (between 96 and 97). The two men are in time reunited, after they have been estranged from each other for an entire season or more:

> How like a winter hath my absence been
> From thee, the pleasure of the fleeting year!
> What freezings have I felt, what dark days seen!
> What old December's bareness everywhere!
> And yet this time removed was summer's time . . .
>
> (97)

> From you have I been absent in the spring,
> When proud-pied April (dressed in all his trim)
> Hath put a spirit of youth in every thing . . .
>   Yet seemed it winter still . . .
>
> (98)

> Rise, resty Muse, my love's sweet face survey,
> If Time have any wrinkle graven there . . .
>
> (100)

The separation has been "dark" and wintry for the poet, and on his return, he wonders whether the passage of time may have affected the youth's beauty and "graven" any wrinkles there. But a reconciliation now takes place, and it appears more secure than at any earlier point in the sequence, including the opening interlude of sonnets 15–19. Indeed, we hear a poetic voice that now sounds "weathered"—acknowledging the passage of time and accepting past faults and betrayals, while regaining once more the confidence that poetry can still celebrate love and even immortalize the young man. In the remarkable sonnets that follow, we find verse that is "golden," tender, and intimate. Sonnet after sonnet yields beautiful lyric passages of a kind not seen before.

If there is an unexpected turn in these poems, it emerges from the fact that they are concerned not only with the youth's beauty, but also with his truth, kindness, and constancy. The friend has reaffirmed his fidelity, enabling the poet to praise him without any trace of the irony or bitterness that characterized so many earlier sonnets. In other words, this group of poems represents a moment, however transient, of renewed mutual love.

The sensitivity to time's passage—and its possible effect on the young man's beauty—is unusually moving, not only in sonnet 100 (quoted above), but especially in 104. The length of the friendship between the two men is now measured in years—and the actual length of remembered experience adds depth to the poet's desire to celebrate the youth:

> To me, fair friend, you never can be old,
> For as you were when first your eye I eyed,
> Such seems your beauty still. Three winters cold
> Have from the forests shook three summers' pride;
> Three beauteous springs to yellow autumn turned
> In process of the seasons have I seen;
> Three April perfumes in three hot Junes burned,
> Since first I saw you fresh, which yet are green.
> Ah yet doth beauty, like a dial hand,
> Steal from his figure, and no pace perceived;

So your sweet hue, which methinks still doth stand,
Hath motion, and mine eye may be deceived;
    For fear of which, hear this thou age unbred:
    Ere you were born was beauty's summer dead.

(104)

The opening lines place all previous episodes in perspective. They focus not on earlier inconstancies, but on the fact that love—and the entrancing nature of the young man—are once again the central subject of the poet and his verse. Nor is there in this poem (or the entire group of sonnets) any trace of self-despising. The poet denigrates neither himself nor his verse (except in the rather conventional, now-familiar mode of sonnets 100–103). The poet's renewed confidence in an ideal of mutual love, together with an increased sense of intimacy, pervades the verse, and this is a new achievement, so to speak. The tone and beauty of so many of these sonnets give expression to a feeling of triumph, and even a few selected passages can convey the sense of a new kind of celebratory verse:

The forward violet thus did I chide:
"Sweet thief, whence didst thou steal thy sweet that
    smells,
If not from my love's breath? . . ."

(99)

Our love was new, and then but in the spring,
When I was wont to greet it with my lays,
As Philomel in summer's front doth sing . . .

(102)

To me, fair friend, you never can be old,
For as you were when first your eye I eyed,
Such seems your beauty still . . .

(104)

Now with the drops of this most balmy time
My love looks fresh, and Death to me subscribes . . .

                                                    (107)

In the last sonnet of this group (108), the poet, for the first
time, defines love explicitly as a mutual exchange between himself and the youth—an exchange between purported equals, even
granting the obvious difference in status between the two:

What's new to speak, what now to register,
That may express my love, or thy dear merit?
Nothing, sweet boy; but yet, like prayers divine,
I must each day say o'er the very same,
Counting no old thing old, thou mine, I thine,
Even as when first I hallowed thy fair name.
So that eternal love in love's fresh case
Weighs not the dust and injury of age . . .

                                                    (108)

The terms of endearment here—"thy dear merit," "sweet boy"—
and the memory of the time "when first I hallowed thy fair name"—
provide the context for the central phrase "thou mine, I thine."
These words are only the poet's, and one may wonder how much
they are mainly an expression of hope rather than of conviction or
fact. But the quality of sustained affection throughout this entire set
of sonnets (97–108) is persuasive, and the restored relationship between the poet and the young man enables the poet to be far more
free in his declaration of reciprocal love. The phrase "thou mine,
I thine" does not—clearly—represent the final word on the subject,
but it does look forward to the similar (yet different and more complex) later attempt on the poet's part to define (after further turmoil)
an ideal of love as "mutual render, only me for thee" (125).

FIFTEEN

Ruined Love

Sonnets 97–108 explored the return of mutual love following the conclusion of the rival poet series. In sonnet 109, however, we discover that the poet has himself been unfaithful, deserting the friend and frequenting "with unknown minds" while giving "to time your own dear-purchased right" (117).

This unexpected fall strikes with singular force, but the structure of the entire sequence makes the poet's transgression more explicable than it may at first seem. Sudden betrayals constitute one pervasive theme of the Sonnets, and mutability (of character and action in the face of Time) is another. Both prepare the way for the poet's susceptibility to the power of desire, and both confirm Time's capacity to alter the course of human affairs. Although the friend has to this point been the unfaithful partner, the poet's relationship with the mistress (discovered as early as sonnet 40) makes him potentially vulnerable to others. No explicit motive is given for the suddenness of the transgression dramatized in sonnets 109–20, but this is consistent with the nature of the friend's early offenses in sonnets 33–35 and 40–42. These sensual betrayals occur swiftly, as if they were mainly manifestations of human nature—subject to chance encounters, inevitable human weakness, or whim and folly.

Other factors are also at work—only hinted at, but persuasive within the confines of the Sonnets' inner logic. At some level, we are ready to understand (and even expect) a reversal of roles, like the recoil of a spring, with the poet now playing a new part, and perhaps taking pleasure in striking back at the friend. In addition—from a structural point of view—the shift does begin to establish the emerging symmetry of the Sonnets as a whole. After the rival poet series and its aftermath, the main focus is on the sensual and other faults of the poet, not the friend. The sequence, in this sense, achieves a growing balance as well as a progression in its sentiments. Now it is the poet who has been "absent," with "others all too near." Later, the subject will once again be the poet's lapses, with a focus on his relationship with the mistress.

Several important characteristics define sonnets 109–20. All are part of a continuing dialogue in which the poet offers one reason after another to explain his offense—often ingenious but unpersuasive rationalizations intended to appease the friend and win back his love. In some, the poet seeks to avoid all or much of the blame for his actions. In others, he simply asks for pity, hoping to be excused and welcomed back by the friend. Later, however, he is seen to be gradually discovering—and understanding—the concepts of fidelity and love at a much deeper level, leading to his effort to bring about another reconciliation with the friend. In effect, the entire movement—from an initial denial of fault, to an acceptance of guilt, to an evolving new concept of fidelity and of love: this movement constitutes the plot of these particular poems, leading to a finale (in 121–26) of all the sonnets devoted to the young man.

•

Although the poet declares (in sonnet 109) that he has never been "false of heart," he begins the next poem by admitting that he has "gone here and there,"

> And made myself a motley to the view,
> Gored mine own thoughts, sold cheap what is most dear,
> Made old offences of affections new.

Most true it is that I have looked on truth
Askance and strangely; but, by all above,
These blenches gave my heart another youth,
And worse essays proved thee my best of love.

(110)

The poet is initially concerned with the way that others view him—as a "motley," or a fool—and this preoccupation will continue to beleaguer him from sonnets 111 and 112 to 121 and 125. Throughout these poems, he seeks a way to distinguish his own identity (including his failings) from that of others whose slander makes him notorious and gives his name a "brand" (111).

At the same time, the first reasons that the poet offers (in 110) for his recent infidelity create the impression that his roaming has been almost casually self-indulgent as well as deliberately designed to injure the friend. His fault has given him "another youth": it has inspired and reawakened passion in him, enabling him to feel liberated. He has looked "on truth / Askance and strangely" rather than deeply. Most of all, his "worse essays" have, in effect, been used as if to "prove" whether the friend is in fact his "best of love." The poet's adventure takes on the character of a self-conscious act to explore "affections new," just as the friend had experimented with new poets in the rival series. This desire to inflict some pain parallels similar assertions in the slightly later sonnet 117, when the poet confesses that he has "hoisted sail to all the winds" while striving to test the "constancy and virtue" of the friend's love. The roles are reversed, but the temptation to wound the other person remains one of the motives that complicates but nevertheless sustains the relationship between the two main figures.

Despite this dynamic, the poet asks (in sonnet 110) to be welcomed back, even "to thy pure and most most loving breast," leading (in 111) to a continuing plea for pity—not forgiveness or pardon, but pity, as if the poet's predicament were not his own fault. Indeed, this is implied in the opening lines of sonnet 111:

O for my sake do you with Fortune chide,
The guilty goddess of my harmful deeds,
That did not better for my life provide
Than public means which public manners breeds.
Thence comes it that my name receives a brand,
And almost thence my nature is subdued
To what it works in, like the dyer's hand.
Pity me then, and wish I were renewed . . .
      Pity me then, dear friend, and I assure ye,
      Even that your pity is enough to cure me.

(111)

Fortune is said to be guilty of the poet's deeds for not having provided him with better means—having condemned him to lead
a "public" life that "public manners breeds." This "almost" compels
him to work, exposed and often ridiculed, in a profession (presumably as a poet, actor, and playwright) that effectively subdues his nature to its demands. Necessity is presented as the main cause of
his offense, although he now offers to do "double penance" to atone
for his deeds (line 12). His pleading—expressed strongly in the
couplet of 111—has an effect on the friend, who appears to respond
sympathetically: sonnet 112 begins to reestablish the relationship
between the two figures.

Your love and pity doth th'impression fill
Which vulgar scandal stamped upon my brow,
For what care I who calls me well or ill,
So you o'er-green my bad, my good allow? . . .
In so profound abysm I throw all care
Of others' voices, that my adder's sense
To critic and to flatterer stopped are . . .
      You are so strongly in my purpose bred
      That all the world besides methinks th'are dead.

(112)

The poet's attempt in this sonnet to banish not only his offenses, but also the opinions of others—while depending solely on the friend's acceptance or criticism of him—is obviously doomed to fail. But it reveals the extent to which the poet's desire for independence from Fortune, "vulgar scandal," and similar forces is an abiding concern, and also demonstrates that a return to the confines of a single love relationship remains his deepest desire: "You are my all the world," he declares (line 5), representing both an assertion of commitment and an effort to distance himself from the realm in which he has transgressed, and where others have the opportunity to slander or revile him.

This inward turn also suggests how much the poet distorts external reality in some of the poems that follow. The shock of his own conduct impedes his capacity to function—which, in turn, leads him to poems of extravagant praise that only underscore his disturbed state of mind. In sonnets 113 and 114, for example, he declares that he has lost the proper function of his eye, has become "partly blind" and has transformed all objects in the external world into images of the young man:

> For if it see the rud'st or gentlest sight,
> The most sweet-favoured or deformed'st creature,
> The mountain, or the sea, the day, or night,
> The crow, or dove, it shapes them to your feature.
> > Incapable of more, replete with you,
> > My most true mind thus maketh mine eye untrue.

(113)

This constant process of metamorphosis—and its curious form of praise—carries over from sonnet 113 to 114, where the poet, "being crowned with you," now claims that even the most monstrous things can be converted by his sight in such a way that "your sweet self resemble." The poet is quick to acknowledge that this is a form of flattery, but it is flattery that—however dangerous—proves to be irresistible. The young man has at least partly responded to the poet's pleas, who now finds himself either "replete" with the friend or "crowned" by him.

In other words, from sonnets 112 to 114, the commitment of love by the poet has begun to emerge in a strong but also distorted form that gains much of its energy from either a rejection of—or transformation of—the outside world. Only in sonnet 115 does the poet return to a more reflective mode that retains an expression of deep love, while also acknowledging—in a crucial and transformative way—that even the most powerful love can be altered and diverted. The poet's early expressions of complete devotion to the friend, which once seemed absolute, are now viewed in retrospect as having been untested and highly vulnerable. His recent transgression has compelled him to confront what he had once scarcely imagined: that he, too, is subject to

> . . . reckoning Time, whose millioned accidents
> Creep in 'twixt vows, and change decrees of kings,
> Tan sacred beauty, blunt the sharp'st intents,
> Divert strong minds to th'course of alt'ring things . . .
>
> (115)

In all the poet's previous poems—even those that seemed to dramatize Time's most threatening powers—he had never abandoned the conviction that Time's effects could somehow be overcome. But now it has crept in "'twixt" his own most fervent vows, and made him subject to "th'course of alt'ring things." Having betrayed the friend, how can he now affirm, persuasively, the ideal of an unwavering faithful love? This is the central question that virtually all the remaining poems in this series attempt to answer, and it is immediately addressed in sonnet 116:

> Let me not to the marriage of true minds
> Admit impediments; love is not love
> Which alters when it alteration finds,

Or bends with the remover to remove.
O no, it is an ever-fixed mark
That looks on tempests and is never shaken;
It is the star to every wand'ring bark,
Whose worth's unknown, although his height be taken.
Love's not Time's fool, though rosy lips and cheeks
Within his bending sickle's compass come;
Love alters not with his brief hours and weeks,
But bears it out even to the edge of doom.
    If this be error and upon me proved,
    I never writ, nor no man ever loved.

(116)

The poet has been debating with himself (and implicitly with the friend). The opening lines suggest that he may doubt whether—in the light of his own infidelity—love can in fact overcome the many "impediments" that stand in the way of a "marriage of true minds." His recent offense—his own broken vows (as well as the friend's)—has compelled him to admit the possibility that an enduring love may simply not be sustainable. In lines 2–6, however, he suddenly declares that devoted and constant love can in fact triumph over all obstacles and endure, because it ultimately has the capacity to remain absolutely firm in spite of the strongest "tempests":

> . . . love is not love
> Which alters when it alteration finds,
> Or bends with the remover to remove.
> O no, it is an ever-fixed mark
> That looks on tempests and is never shaken . . .

(116)

These lines seem confident in their assertion of the overriding power of love, but at the same time they also appear to be an attempt by the poet to strengthen his *own* assertion that no "alterations" or lapses should finally stand in the way of an enduring love and deep commitment. Much earlier in the sequence, a far less experienced and hopeful poet had written (in sonnet 25):

> Then happy I that love and am beloved
> Where I may not remove, nor be removed.

> (25)

Now (in sonnet 116) love has been confronted and disrupted by very potent forces, but is nevertheless said to survive despite all "tempests" and vicissitudes. This conception of an indomitable love— emerging from an ultimate refusal to "remove"—is new to the Sonnets. Love is no longer focused on beauty, nor does it assume invariable constancy. Rather, it has the character of a self-sufficient force, dependent upon willpower and determination. Indeed, it can survive "even to the edge of doom." At the same time, there is no longer any claim that the poet's love or the image of the beloved can be "eternized" in verse that will itself be imperishable.

If there are problems with sonnet 116, they arise from the fact that the poet's unqualified confidence in the power of love derives primarily from his own declarations, and these seem strained from the very beginning. In fact, we can sense throughout the verse an overemphatic stress on love's invulnerable power, with little or no explanation of how this invulnerability might be sustained:

> Let me not to the marriage . . .
> . . . love is not love
> Which alters . . .
> O no, it is an ever-fixed mark . . .
> Love alters not . . .

> (116)

The tone varies but the lines remain insistent and even exclamatory in the poet's effort to persuade himself (as well as the friend). The sonnet's rhetorical forcefulness reminds us that the voice we hear is "dramatic" insofar as it attempts to respond to all the extraordinary pressures and difficulties of the poet's situation following his fall.

Sonnet 119 builds upon 116, capturing vividly the pain of the poet's confrontation with guilt as well as the agitation of his experience with "madness." His anguish derives partly from a conscious sense of moral self-betrayal, and partly from his inability to control the lust that has driven him:

> Applying fears to hopes, and hopes to fears,
> Still losing when I saw myself to win!
> What wretched errors hath my heart committed,
> Whilst it hath thought itself so blessed never!
> How have mine eyes out of their spheres been fitted
> In the distraction of this madding fever!
>
> (119)

These lines bring us as close to the delirium of desire as we will find in the entire first section of the Sonnets: the poet "loses" when he had sought to win, and has committed "wretched errors" while having hoped to be "blessed" in the possession of his new love. He can perceive and anatomize the contradictions of his situation, but as long as his "fever" lasts, he finds himself helpless. The way out of this apparently hopeless cycle of desire and disillusion lies in the poet's ability to understand his predicament as well as his capacity to convert its very contradictions into a source of renewal. After returning to the friend, his love appears to be stronger precisely because it has survived and even grown despite the near-mortal blow he has dealt it:

> O benefit of ill: now I find true
> That better is by evil still made better,
> And ruined love when it is built anew
> Grows fairer than at first, more strong, far greater.

So I return rebuked to my content,
And gain by ills thrice more than I have spent.

(119)

The poet invokes the concept of the "fortunate fall"—evil enabling a yet more powerful good to come into being. The argument may be persuasive, or perhaps simply too convenient—close to rationalization. The proposition in the last line seems particularly forced. Whatever we conclude, however, a major advance beyond the poet's stance in sonnets 109–15 (as well as 117–18) has been achieved. Not only has there been an acceptance of guilt and a dramatization of the poet's "distraction," but he has also asserted (in 116) the unyielding nature of love, and suggested (in 119) how love may in fact gain greater strength as a result of human frailty. Although the poet no longer claims that either the image of the beloved's beauty (or the power of his own verse) will survive eternally, his compensation for this loss is the growing conviction that love—now defined in terms of an unshakable fidelity—will be able to withstand the assaults of Time and of "slanderers," and any "removals" that it may encounter.

•

Sonnet 120 closes this series (109–20) and reveals unexpected shifts of tone that color the entire poem:

That you were once unkind befriends me now,
And for that sorrow which I then did feel
Needs must I under my transgression bow,
Unless my nerves were brass or hammered steel.
For if you were by my unkindness shaken
As I by yours, y'have passed a hell of time,
And I, a tyrant, have no leisure taken
To weigh how once I suffered in your crime.
O that our night of woe might have rememb'red
My deepest sense, how hard true sorrow hits,

And soon to you, as you to me then tend'red
The humble salve which wounded bosom fits!
    But that your trespass now becomes a fee;
    Mine ransoms yours, and yours must ransom me.

(120)

The friend's very first, and shocking, transgression (in 33–34) has left so indelible a mark that it remains the "offence" to which the poet now returns. The distance—in time and presumably space—that the poet now places between himself and the friend ("For if you were" and "I . . . have no leisure taken") implies that there has been a gap in contact between the two figures, leaving the poet uncertain—and somewhat unconcerned?—about how the young man has finally reacted to the infidelity. Moreover, the poet seems, like a "tyrant," to have consciously (and cruelly?) enjoyed playing a disengaged role.

This sense of distance is, however, juxtaposed with altogether different passages of intimacy and much greater depth of feeling. Ultimately, the poet remembers the sorrow he had himself experienced when first abandoned, and says that he "must" respond sympathetically, "Unless my nerves were brass or hammered steel." And then he regrets not having immediately reached out to the friend:

O that our night of woe might have rememb'red
My deepest sense, how hard true sorrow hits . . .

(120)

These lines lead to another reunion based on the shared "woe" of "our" past events: a reunion deriving from the fact that each has suffered "a hell of time." Yet in the concluding couplet, the tone and values suddenly alter once again:

But that your trespass now becomes a fee;
Mine ransoms yours, and yours must ransom me.

(120)

The introduction of a form of bargain—similar ransoms for similar fees—returns us to a worldly space where the intrusion of argument and rhetoric impinge upon, but do not entirely vitiate, the move to rebuild love on the basis of sympathetic understanding. The poet's betrayal is unexpectedly viewed as a payment for the friend's, and the friend's now "must ransom me." The "must" is implicitly coercive, and the young man is asked for something that is effectively a quid pro quo.

In spite of these qualifications, the reconciliation results in the affirmations that soon follow (122, 123–25). Having passed through his own recent fall, and having recalled the earlier reunion marked by the friend's spontaneous tears of sympathy and regret (34), the poet feels not only reunited with the friend, but actually emboldened. He has already asserted that "ruined love" can be built anew. Now he is prepared to celebrate love and his own constancy as if they fully possessed the formidable and independent power that he first described in sonnet 116.

SIXTEEN

Hugely Politic

Nearly all of the sonnets from 121 to 125 are among the most declarative and confident in the entire sequence. The poet is seeking to prevail over powerful forces kept at bay by the sheer strength of rhetoric and proclaimed conviction. He is striving, in effect, to achieve an act of self-definition and self-affirmation. Indeed, the main focus in three of these five sonnets is on the poet's commitment to a mode of constancy that can withstand all that is arrayed against it.

In sonnet 121, he moves to distinguish himself from those who have impugned him through rumor and slander:

> For why should others' false adulterate eyes
> Give salutation to my sportive blood?
> Or on my frailties why are frailer spies,
> Which in their wills count bad what I think good?
> No, I am that I am, and they that level
> At my abuses reckon up their own;
> I may be straight though they themselves be bevel;
> By their rank thoughts my deeds must not be shown . . .
>
> (121)

The poet's claim is not that he is free of faults—his "blood" is "sportive," he has "frailties," he is associated with "abuses," and—

far from impeccable—he suggests that he "may be straight" but is not necessarily so. He claims only a degree of virtue that the "vile" (line 1) do not possess, distancing himself from the false accusations of those who despise him, who view him as an outcast, and who "brand" his name. "I am that I am" is a statement of self-vindication as well as one of confession. It sets the stage for the following poems, which stress his capacity to place himself outside the realms of "policy," of "thrivers," of slanderers and "informers," and—for the term of life—outside Time itself.

Sonnet 123 insists that Time will never be able to "boast that I do change": "I will be true despite thy scythe and thee." And these assurances lead directly to the very great sonnet 124:

> If my dear love were but the child of state,
> It might for Fortune's bastard be unfathered,
> As subject to Time's love, or to Time's hate,
> Weeds among weeds, or flowers with flowers gathered.
> No, it was builded far from accident;
> It suffers not in smiling pomp, nor falls
> Under the blow of thralled discontent,
> Whereto th'inviting time our fashion calls.
> It fears not Policy, that heretic,
> Which works on leases of short-numb'red hours,
> But all alone stands hugely politic,
> That it nor grows with heat, nor drowns with show'rs.
>   To this I witness call the fools of Time,
>   Which die for goodness, who have lived for crime.

(124)

Love is now the ruling power, no longer subject to Time's "accidents" or to the rewards that Fortune might bestow. The reference to Time links the poem to 123, but there is also an obvious shift in emphasis from Time to Fortune—to the hazards of social and political existence, dominated essentially by the unpredictable turnings of Fortune's wheel. Because the poet's abiding love is said to have been nourished far from the world of intrigue—"smiling pomp" and "thralled discontent"—it is simply not subject to their whims. It is also removed from "policy"—from scheming individuals and their actions, which exert so strong an influence on the "fashion" of the day. Indeed, Policy (a heretic in relation to true values and commitments) lives purely in the present, by means of short leases and equally "short-numb'red hours." The poet's love, by contrast, stands "all alone," unchanging in its nature, and therefore "hugely politic": it has its own form of "policy"—as if it were an independent state with its own governing laws and values, immune to the influences of the ordinary world of mutability. As witnesses, the poet calls on those who have allowed themselves to be fools of Time: they have lived "for crime" (for perverted values) and their deaths highlight the very different nature of goodness.

In this and other ways, sonnet 124 is a proclamation of the poet's own unalterable constancy, irrespective of the surrounding world. In sonnet 125, the theme of inviolable fidelity continues. The context relates closely to that of 124 and is linked to it as a companion:

Were't aught to me I bore the canopy,
With my extern the outward honouring,
Or laid great bases for eternity,
Which proves more short than waste or ruining?
Have I not seen dwellers on form and favour
Lose all, and more, by paying too much rent,
For compound sweet forgoing simple savour,
Pitiful thrivers, in their gazing spent?

(125)

The focus is again on the false values of society, in which "thriving" reigns, and where the effort to succeed in worldly affairs is seen as "paying too much rent." Bearing a "canopy" to honor those of high birth clearly constitutes homage to the outward trappings of power and privilege. If there is to be "obsequiousness"—paying homage to another—it can be only in relation to inner values where love and fidelity can be found:

> No, let me be obsequious in thy heart,
> And take thou my oblation, poor but free,
> Which is not mixed with seconds, knows no art
> But mutual render, only me for thee.
>   Hence, thou suborned informer! A true soul
>   When most impeached stands least in thy control.

> (125)

The realm in which "honouring" and the right form of thriving should take place is in the sphere where the heart resides. There, the speaker has nothing to offer (and nothing to seek) in worldly terms: his gift is necessarily poor and also free. "Oblation" sets the tone for the devoted seriousness of the artless ceremony to be fulfilled through a form of marriage: "mutual render, only me for thee."

Previous attempts to describe such "a marriage of true minds" between the poet and the friend have been qualified, or have fallen short: the "perfect ceremony of love's rite" (23); "thou mine, I thine" (108); "Let me not to the marriage of true minds / Admit impediments" (116); "Mine ransoms yours, and yours must ransom me" (120). In 125, there is a generosity of spirit in which the poet gives (and subordinates) himself, together with an asserted conception of genuine equality in love. Although he acknowledges the dominant position of the young friend ("let me be obsequious") and freely offers himself to the other ("take thou my oblation"), he appears to have arrived at a hallowed place where mutual render can in fact occur, although there is no assurance that these offerings will be accepted.

The poem remains a plea ("let me," "take thou") and we have no indication of how the young man may respond. Then the couplet, with its intrusion of the "suborned informer," suggests that even so moving a plea can be threatened (even falsified) by those who inhabit the world of policy and thriving. The poet rebuffs the informer, but the very encounter reveals that there is no way for him to completely separate the world of policy (or slander, or mutability) from that in which he claims to be "hugely politic."

This fact in itself raises another question: to what extent has the poet—as chosen writer and celebrant—escaped bearing the "canopy" in relation to the friend? Has he not been implicated in honoring "the outward" or external aspects of existence, including his continued quest to remain the young man's favored poet? Various onlookers in the Sonnets—including the "spies" in 121, in addition to slanderers and the "suborned informer" of 125—may well view the poet as a "thriver" and flatterer, seeking to make his way in precisely the manner that he decries. Yet, however much the poet may value his role as the friend's chosen writer, and however much flattery there may be in many sonnets to the friend, the actual power of the poet's love and his abiding devotion to the young man is so strongly and persuasively expressed that it transcends mere worldly considerations. The poet is far from immune (as we see, for example, in 29 and 121 and other sonnets) to ambition and a variety of frailties and temptations, but these never dominate his willingness to suffer whatever pain and humiliation love may bring him. He remains constant throughout, even in the poems that record his own inconstancy.

The vigor of the protestations in sonnets 121–25 is in one sense convincing, but the rhetoric of assertion is also disconcerting, as if the poet's doubts were driving him toward extreme self-certainty. The repeated exclamations add to this impression: "No, I am that I am"; "No! Time, thou shalt not boast"; "No, it was builded far from accident"; "No, let me be obsequious in thy heart"—all of which recall sonnet 116, "O no, it is an ever-fixed mark." These are the cries of someone who remains mutable and vulnerable, in spite of his determination to affirm a vision of unalterable love that can exist irrespective of Time and its dominion.

•

If sonnets 123–25 are dedicated to the concept of an unalterable love, they have—as suggested—also passed well beyond the poet's earlier effort to "eternize" the young man (and his beauty), or declare that his own verse will be imperishable. Instead, there is a paradoxical admission that constancy in love can—during the course of one's existence—overcome mutability, while simultaneously recognizing that Time will eventually triumph: "Our dates are brief," says the poet in sonnet 123, and it is wiser to ignore Time's "registers" of either the present or the past, since these are inevitably misleading. At the end of the sonnet, the poet (addressing Time) declares that "I will be true despite thy scythe and thee."

This acceptance of mortality, with its recognition that "eternity" is beyond the limits of the poet's capacity, affects the tone and denouement of sonnet 122, where the poet concedes that he has given away a gift of "tables" from the friend, because their words are now inscribed in his memory:

> Thy gift, thy tables, are within my brain
> Full charactered with lasting memory,
> Which shall above that idle rank remain
> Beyond all date, even to eternity;
> Or, at the least, so long as brain and heart
> Have faculty by nature to subsist;
> Till each to razed oblivion yield his part
> Of thee, thy record never can be missed.

(122)

The tone is subdued. The poet first asserts that his memory will guard the friend's gift "even to eternity," but he then shifts to "at the least" until "razed oblivion" or death. This move (and the giving of tables) may signal that the relationship between the poet and the friend is coming to a close, although such a view is difficult to reconcile with sonnets 119–20 and 123–25. Alternatively, the sonnet's sobriety may reflect the fact that hopes and aspirations related to "eternity" have now given way to a conception of love that is ultimately subject to the ravages of Time.

Such an alternative seems clearly at the heart of the rhymed-couplet "sonnet" 126 (which has just twelve lines):

> O thou my lovely boy, who in thy power
> Dost hold Time's fickle glass, his sickle hour;
> Who hast by waning grown, and therein show'st
> Thy lovers withering, as thy sweet self grow'st;
> If Nature (sovereign mistress over wrack),
> As thou goest onwards still will pluck thee back,
> She keeps thee to this purpose, that her skill
> May Time disgrace, and wretched minutes kill.
> Yet fear her, O thou minion of her pleasure,
> She may detain, but not still keep, her treasure!
> Her audit (though delayed) answered must be,
> And her quietus is to render thee.
>
> (126)

This is in part a tender poem ("my lovely boy") and it begins by praising the youth's power to "grow" while others wither and wane. Indeed, he appears to be stronger than Time itself. But we soon learn that it is actually Nature who shields the boy—keeping him for herself while also demonstrating that she can "disgrace" Time by keeping it at bay. This effort, however, is purely illusory: neither loveliness nor youth can ultimately be sustained, and there is no movement by the poet to suggest that he and his verse can "eternize" the young man. Nature can "detain" but not "keep her treasure": in the end, she must surrender him.

The duel with Time and Death has been lost; beauty itself counts for little; inevitability and necessity reign. Only unalterable love may still survive—during the course of life itself.

SEVENTEEN

Past Cure

Following the 126 sonnets addressed to the young man, there is a group of 25 addressed to the mistress. This shift introduces an obvious division in the sequence and, simultaneously, a fulfillment of expectations that reinforces the design of the Sonnets as a whole. These 25 poems deal mainly with the poet's lust for his mistress, but their images are closely related to those of sonnets 109–20 (when the poet deserted his friend in order to seek "others"). In 109–20, we find allusions to "all frailties" that "besiege . . . blood"; "appetite" that "grinds"; blindness that "parts" the very "function" of the eyes; a desire for "bitter sauces" that make one "diseased"; and finally Sirens, "limbecks foul as hell," "eyes out of their spheres"—and the "distraction of this madding fever." For example:

> . . . in my nature reigned
> All frailties that besiege all kinds of blood . . .
>
> (109)

> Mine appetite I never more will grind
> On newer proof . . .
>
> (110)

> Since I left you, mine eye is in my mind;
> And that which governs me to go about

Doth part his function, and is partly blind,
Seems seeing, but effectually is out . . .

(113)

To bitter sauces did I frame my feeding,
And, sick of welfare, found a kind of meetness
To be diseased . . .

(118)

What potions have I drunk of Siren tears
Distilled from limbecks foul as hell within . . .
How have mine eyes out of their spheres been fitted
In the distraction of this madding fever!

(119)

Passages such as these are unique in the first section of the sequence, and they lead us directly to the language of several poems addressed to the mistress:

Thou blind fool, Love, what dost thou to mine eyes,
That they behold and see not what they see?

(137)

For if I should despair I should grow mad,
And in my madness might speak ill of thee;
Now this ill-wresting world is grown so bad,
Mad slanderers by mad ears believed be.

(140)

My love is as a fever longing still
For that which longer nurseth the disease,
Feeding on that which doth preserve the ill,
Th'uncertain sickly appetite to please . . .
Past cure I am, now reason is past care,
And frantic mad with evermore unrest;

My thoughts and my discourse as madmen's are . . .
    For I have sworn thee fair, and thought thee
      bright,
    Who art as black as hell, as dark as night.

                                                  (147)

O me! what eyes hath love put in my head,
Which have no correspondence with true sight?

                                                (148)

The images from the first group of sonnets look forward to the second, helping to bind together the two main sections of the sequence, although there are important differences as well as a progression from one set to the other. The initial group is comparatively controlled: descriptive statements prevail, and the only exclamatory lines come toward the very end. In the second group, an agitated voice is present from the beginning, while questions and exclamations follow rapidly upon one another. In other words, the poet's first intense encounter with desire and passion (in 109–20) has soon led to his complete subjugation by lust.

The sonnets to the mistress—whose beauty is said to be dark or "black"—begin with a poem (127) that functions as a counterpoint to the very first sonnet in the sequence ("From fairest creatures we desire increase"), and it sets the stage for much that follows:

In the old age black was not counted fair,
Or if it were it bore not beauty's name;
But now is black beauty's successive heir,
And beauty slandered with a bastard shame:
For since each hand hath put on Nature's power,
Fairing the foul with art's false borrowed face,
Sweet beauty hath no name, no holy bower,
But is profaned, if not lives in disgrace.

                                                (127)

The poem introduces us to an entirely new realm. Fairness and beauty have been superseded: beauty has been "slandered" with "a bastard shame," and indeed has no place, no "holy bower," that is her own. The use of artifice—cosmetics—creates an entirely novel conception: true (ideal) beauty exists in memory and, in this sense, remains a vital part of the poet's consciousness. It is, however, only a reminder of a vanished universe. He soon embraces what is "black"—"art's false borrowed face"—and later discovers that there are others who believe that all "beauty should look so." There was a prefiguration of this situation in sonnets 67–68, where "false painting" and "bastard signs of fair" were used by others to imitate the beauty of the young man. Now, however, the effort is not to imitate fairness but to envision "blackness" itself as a new ideal. The poet recognizes this inversion, but he soon finds himself—in a move toward radical self-deception—drawn to "art's false borrowed face" and its purported beauty.

•

Sonnets 127–54 are divided into well-defined sections, from poems that plead for the mistress's love (127–37), to those which define a mutually deceitful relationship (138–46), and then to a final group (147–52) in which the poet struggles to articulate, in increasingly strident terms, the extremity of his state of mind. In desperation, he finds himself enslaved by lust, unable to choose what is best over what is worst. Although this problem is intrinsic to many of the mistress sonnets, it simply becomes more powerful and insistent at the very end.

The opening set of sonnets to the mistress—some playful, some pleading, some more revelatory—portray the poet in different roles, all intended to win her love. In 128, he watches her playing a musical instrument, wishing that her fingers might touch not the instrument's wood, but his own hand and lips. In 130, he insists that the mistress is no "goddess" and refuses to use elaborate poetic ornament (similes and metaphors of "false compare") to describe her. When she walks, she is thoroughly human and "treads on the ground," but he nevertheless believes her to be "as rare" as any woman. In 132, he suggests that her eyes wear black because they may pity his pain and torment:

> O let it then as well beseem thy heart
> To mourn for me, since mourning doth thee grace,
> And suit thy pity like in every part.
> > Then will I swear beauty herself is black,
> > And all they foul that thy complexion lack.
>
> > > (132)

The poet's plea for the mistress's heart (as well as her eyes) to pity him leads him to "swear" that "beauty herself is black." He will, in effect, surrender to her, although the need to swear—and to describe complexions other than hers as "foul"—suggests the somewhat forced and fateful nature of taking such a step. Moreover, this poem follows a similar sonnet to "blackness" (131), which raises even more serious questions. It begins as a parody of a conventional Petrarchan sonnet—a type ordinarily addressed to a lady who is beautiful and virtuous, and whose inaccessibility is often characterized by her lover as cruelty:

> Thou art as tyrannous, so as thou art,
> As those whose beauties proudly make them cruel;
> For well thou know'st to my dear doting heart
> Thou art the fairest and most precious jewel.
> Yet in good faith some say that thee behold,
> Thy face hath not the power to make love groan;
> To say they err, I dare not be so bold,
> Although I swear it to myself alone.
> And to be sure that is not false I swear,
> A thousand groans but thinking on thy face
> One on another's neck do witness bear

Thy black is fairest in my judgement's place.
>   In nothing art thou black save in thy deeds,
>   And thence this slander as I think proceeds.

(131)

The lady is not merely cruel but tyrannous in a willful and con-sciously pointed way. The poet offers not a conventional lover's sighs, laments, or renewed appeals, but a "thousand groans" in a display of helpless "doting" that reveals the powerlessness of his state, in the face of her rejection.

The unexpected turn in the poem comes in the suggestion that others do not share his view of the mistress, and certainly not his feelings. He is sufficiently uncertain not to disagree publicly, although he does so privately. He also feels the need to prove to himself that what he has sworn—that the mistress's "black is fairest"—is in fact true. Given his confirmation, one expects a compliment or further expression of devotion in the couplet, but instead he offers an indictment that seems—momentarily—to ally the poet with the "slanderers":

> In nothing art thou black save in thy deeds,
> And thence this slander as I think proceeds.

(131)

The allusion to black deeds reflects her unwillingness to yield to the poet, and perhaps suggests her willingness to give herself to many others (a point mentioned as early as sonnets 134–38). In either case, two significant events have taken place in sonnet 131. The poet—however tentatively—has been compelled to wonder whether his view of the "black" mistress's beauty (and her other qualities) is a partial and purely subjective one. In addition, he has been driven not simply to implore her, but to begin to revile her. Two of the major themes of the sonnets to the mistress have been sounded, and will affect the tone and texture of all that follows.

In sonnets 133–34, the mistress's relationship with the poet's friend is revealed, providing another important link between the two main parts of the sequence. These poems are, however, dramatically different from the analogous earlier sonnets, 40–42, when it was the friend who took assertive possession of the mistress. Now the dark lady is the dominant figure, in full control. The poet makes this abundantly clear (in 133):

> Beshrew that heart that makes my heart to groan
> For that deep wound it gives my friend and me.
> Is't not enough to torture me alone,
> But slave to slavery my sweet'st friend must be?
>
> (133)

Here, the friend is not only "tortured," but he—like the poet— has become a "slave" to the mistress. Indeed, much of the struggle relates to the poet's effort to free the friend from the mistress's bondage. But this proves impossible, as we discover in sonnet 134: not only is the mistress tyrannical, but the friend is described as "kind"—that is to say, compliant. He chooses to remain her captive, and this constitutes another (and final) act of dispossession and usurpation in the sequence. The mistress has stripped the poet of virtually all that he still retained:

> Me from myself thy cruel eye hath taken,
> And my next self thou harder hast engrossed;
> Of him, myself, and thee I am forsaken . . .
>
> (133)

This acknowledgment marks the extent to which both the poet and the friend are now enslaved, in moral as well as sensual terms. The loss of "self" leads directly to the unrestrained sexuality and blindness that are the central themes of the next two poems. Sonnets 135 and 136 complement each other: both are witty, but nevertheless deeply serious in their undertones. Their extravagant use of sexual puns makes a case in favor of unrestrained copulation. The mistress is

now known to be accessible to many who desire nothing more than
sexual pleasure, and in so doing, she exercises her will in ways that
are either lavish and open, or else utterly closed. The poet, having
been denied, tries several different arguments on his own behalf—
the first of which involves puns on the word *will* (including *Will*):

> Wilt thou, whose will is large and spacious,
> Not once vouchsafe to hide my will in thine?
> Shall will in others seem right gracious,
> And in my will no fair acceptance shine?

(135)

> Thus far for love, my love-suit, sweet, fulfil.
> Will will fulfil the treasure of thy love,
> Ay, fill it full with wills, and my will one.

(136)

The pleas in these two poems indicate how far the poet has fallen.
Nor does he meet with success: the mistress remains unyielding,
and the tone gives way to self-accusatory verse in which the poet
tries to account for his "blindness"—for his swift decline into lust,
and for his ever-deepening self-corruption:

> Thou blind fool, Love, what dost thou to mine eyes,
> That they behold and see not what they see?
> They know what beauty is, see where it lies,
> Yet what the best is take the worst to be.
> If eyes, corrupt by over-partial looks,
> Be anchored in the bay where all men ride,
> Why of eyes' falsehood hast thou forged hooks,
> Whereto the judgement of my heart is tied? . . .
> > In things right true my heart and eyes have erred,
> > And to this false plague are they now transferred.

(137)

This is the first sonnet to the mistress in which the poet acknowledges that his eyes—knowing the difference between true beauty and its opposite—cannot resist choosing the "false plague." Earlier, in sonnet 131, the poet had admitted that "some say" the mistress is not so beautiful as to make hearts "groan," but this view was soon set aside. Now, having experienced the feelings and events of sonnets 133–34 and the slide toward uninhibited sexual passion in 135–36, the poet's moral values come briefly to the fore, challenging the fact that his eyes know "what the best is" but nevertheless choose "the worst": they put "fair truth upon so foul a face," and thereby commit two errors. They seem to see things correctly and yet they consistently distort them; and then, even when they see clearly, without distortion, they are invariably propelled by desire, failing to choose "things right true." The poet now recognizes that his eyes have been corrupted by "over-partial looks"—they are false, but his feelings nevertheless drive him to the "bay where all men ride." Most of all, a full "transferral" of his heart and eyes takes place at the very end of sonnet 137. The poet gives himself entirely to the "blind fool, Love" and its "false plague." This is a fatal and absolute decision. While there will be future moments of doubt and deep self-questioning, nothing hereafter deflects the poet's headlong movement to "shun the heaven that leads men to this hell" (129).

•

Once this final commitment or "transferral" to lust has been made—and once the mistress has finally accepted the poet—the next group of poems focuses primarily on different ways in which the relationship between the two lovers is built upon self-deception and self-corruption. The subject of sonnet 138 is willful mutual lying. The poet remains concerned about his advancing age, but he now shows none of the anxiety that was constantly on his mind in the sonnets to the young man. Instead, he treats the topic in a cool, unruffled way:

Thus vainly thinking that she thinks me young,
Although she knows my days are past the best,
Simply I credit her false-speaking tongue:
On both sides thus is simple truth suppressed . . .
    Therefore I lie with her, and she with me,
    And in our faults by lies we flattered be.

(138)

If the first 125 sonnets of the sequence revealed an effort, however compromised, to achieve truth-telling and avoid flattery, these later poems have reached a point where flattery and lies are intrinsic—and consciously so—to the relationship between the two main figures. Neither party believes what the other is saying. "Simple truth" is now willingly "suppressed"—an echo of (and contrast to) the poet's earlier lament (in sonnet 66) that "simple truth" is wrongfully called "simplicity." The pun in line 13 of sonnet 138 only underscores the fact that there is no more truth in the now-established sexual union than in any other aspect of the relationship. A clear-eyed perversion of values has become the norm.

After sonnet 138, the poet moves further into the realm of deceit: sonnets 139 and 140 acknowledge that the mistress loves an uncertain number of others, but the poet insists that she should act as though no other loves exist. Fidelity and constancy are now completely undermined:

Tell me thou lov'st elsewhere; but in my sight,
Dear heart, forbear to glance thine eye aside . . .

(139)

This sonnet ends with a decision to forgive the mistress, and to resolve (with obvious wit) the difficulties that have arisen. But in the very next poem, the poet's frustration, leading quickly to anger and threats, breaks through the surface:

Be wise as thou art cruel, do not press
My tongue-tied patience with too much disdain,
Lest sorrow lend me words, and words express
The manner of my pity-wanting pain.
If I might teach thee wit, better it were,
Though not to love, yet, love, to tell me so—
As testy sick men, when their deaths be near,
No news but health from their physicians know.
For if I should despair I should grow mad,
And in my madness might speak ill of thee;
Now this ill-wresting world is grown so bad,
Mad slanderers by mad ears believed be.
     That I may not be so, nor thou belied,
     Bear thine eyes straight, though thy proud heart
       go wide.

(140)

The tone—suddenly commanding in the opening lines—becomes near-desperate in the last quatrain and couplet. The poet wants the mistress to act as if she loves him and he will presumably "believe" what she says in exactly the same false way that she does. But the possibility of the poet's actual "despair" is new—and the sense of impending madness that would result (from an explicit sign of waywardness on her part) is far more tortured than anything encountered before. Indeed, it marks a new level of barely controlled feeling that leads (in the last few lines) to potential revenge in the form of deliberate slander. This is doubly ironic: not only is it a "mad" perversion of values, but it threatens to subject the mistress to the spite (of being "belied" by slanderers) that the poet himself has experienced throughout so much of the sequence.

The movement to acknowledged mutual deception, self-conscious lying, and even forms of revenge reaches deeper levels by sonnet 142. In the first lines, the poet suggests, "Love is my sin" and that his love is "grounded on sinful loving." His love of the mistress is utterly tainted, and we soon learn that professed love and vows are given and relinquished with ease by both figures. When the mistress appears to condemn or "hate" the poet's "sinful loving," he replies:

> O but with mine compare thou thine own state,
> And thou shalt find it merits not reproving,
> Or if it do, not from those lips of thine,
> That have profaned their scarlet ornaments,
> And sealed false bonds of love as oft as mine,
> Robbed others' beds' revenues of their rents.
> Be it lawful I love thee as thou lov'st those
> Whom thine eyes woo as mine importune thee.

(142)

If the poet is to be reproved, then it should clearly not be by the mistress, because she is guilty of "profaning" her lips (with "false bonds" or vows) "as oft as mine." Both figures are guilty, and the mistress has gone so far as to rob "others' beds' revenues of their rents." In short, the pattern of lies and broken vows has become increasingly intricate: there is not only the mutual deceit between poet and mistress, but also the mistress's conscious deceit and "robbery" of others. Indeed, vows—so important in the first 125 poems of the sequence—have now become common—and commonly broken. At the time of the poet's very first defeat by the power of passion (sonnet 115), the recognition that Time could in fact "Creep in 'twixt vows" came as a revelation and shock. Now that earlier fault of the poet—and the current behavior of the mistress—have become habitual.

Sonnet 141 was the first poem (among those addressed to the mistress) to mention the word *sin* (in its very last line), followed (in 142) by the poet's admission that "Love is my sin." These two poems introduce a small group in which a number of religious terms (such as "evil," "saint," "devil," "fiend," and "soul") appear, but are ordinarily used either in passing or in the self-consciously exaggerated manner of 144. Their cumulative effect, however, is to prepare us for sonnet 146, which is by far the most somber, reflective, and spiritual poem among the final twenty-five:

> Poor soul, the center of my sinful earth,
> Feeding these rebel pow'rs that thee array,
> Why dost thou pine within and suffer dearth,
> Painting thy outward walls so costly gay?
> Why so large cost, having so short a lease,
> Dost thou upon thy fading mansion spend?
> Shall worms, inheritors of this excess,
> Eat up thy charge? Is this thy body's end?
> Then, soul, live thou upon thy servant's loss,
> And let that pine to aggravate thy store;
> Buy terms divine in selling hours of dross;
> Within be fed, without be rich no more:
> > So shalt thou feed on death, that feeds on men,
> > And death once dead, there's no more dying then.
>
> (146)

This sonnet resembles a very few others in the sequence in which the poet's expression of feelings and thoughts reflects depths of experience well beyond the poem's immediate context. The questioning, meditative tone—the confession of perplexity, and the poet's tenderness concerning his "poor soul"—all serve as a commentary on his diminished, vulnerable state as he faces the "rebel pow'rs that thee array." His fading mansion is an obvious symbol of excess, and the steady interrogation (from lines 3–6) is not so much a forceful exhortation to the soul to regenerate itself, as it is a form of decrescendo, amounting to near-surrender. The final lines, moreover, simply lack the energy of conviction: we do not expect a future change on the poet's part.

Sonnet 146 interrupts the surface drama that is taking place, and gives expression to what—in terms of profound values and earlier ideals—the poet has lost. If it had been at all possible to escape from the passions that have entrapped him, this would have been the moment. But not only does the poem end in effective defeat, it leads directly to the sequence's final group of sonnets (147–54), in which the poet immediately acknowledges that

> My reason, the physician to my love,
> Angry that his prescriptions are not kept,
> Hath left me, and I desperate, now approve
> Desire is death, which physic did except.
> Past cure I am, now reason is past care . . .
>
> (147)

"Poor soul" marks a point of no return, and the poet recognizes in sonnet 147 that "Desire is death"—a form of death he cannot evade. Indeed, by the end of this sonnet, he moves much further than before in the direction of "madness," including an exceptionally forceful condemnation of the mistress:

> My thoughts and my discourse as madmen's are,
> At random from the truth vainly expressed:
>   For I have sworn thee fair, and thought thee
>   bright,
>   Who art as black as hell, as dark as night.
>
> (147)

This moment has the effect of a revelation, and it parallels—with obvious significant differences—the moment of recognition that the poet experienced much earlier—in the sonnets to the friend—when he was driven (in 95–96) to acknowledge how much his eyes had deceived him, and how much the appearance of a certain form of beauty (the friend's fairness, in contrast to the mistress's dark-ness) had so often misled him. The crisis in both main sections of the sequence involves the poet's realization that he has consciously allowed himself to love (in contrary but irresistible ways) beyond what seems to be a reversible point. In each case, the poet's eyes have been "perjured" (152): they have refused to acknowledge what they plainly see, and in each case a form of passion has bound the poet in a way that has left him powerless. In the son-nets to the mistress, the poet's self-deceit takes him far beyond anything that we encounter in the poems to the young man. Nevertheless, the two parts of the sequence are linked to each other in this way, despite the fact that the poet "recovers" in son-nets 119–20 and 121–25, in contrast to his steady dissolution in 147–52.

•

The very last few sonnets to the mistress dramatize the poet's in-capacity to discover any "correspondence" between what he sees (and swears to) concerning the mistress's "beauty" and even "truth" (152), and—by contrast—what the world appears to see. Beyond this initial discordance, the poet is of course divided within him-self: he knows that the mistress is false—unfaithful, untruthful, unkind—and yet he cannot help desiring her.

In other words, the entire set of sonnets to the mistress pro-gresses from early poems where the poet declares that she is "as rare / As any she belied with false compare" (130) and is "the fairest and most precious jewel" (131); to an admission of past blindness, as in sonnet 137, where the poet "knows what beauty is" but admits that "In things right true my heart and eyes have erred"; to a final point where the mistress is seen as "black as hell" (147), characterized by "foul faults" (148), or "defects" (149) that are, ironically, a source of attraction as well as condemnation. This perversion—that the poet should love what others (and he him-self) despise—begins to hold "sway" over him with "pow'rful might" (150). He finds himself so deeply enmeshed that he can only pose questions, while giving expression to his bewilderment, torment, and horror:

> Who taught thee how to make me love thee more,
> The more I hear and see just cause of hate?
> O, though I love what others do abhor,
> With others thou shouldst not abhor my state:
>> If thy unworthiness raised love in me,
>> More worthy I to be beloved of thee.
>
> (150)

If one loves what one actually hates, suggesting that it is the very "unworthiness" of the loved one that is attractive, there remains only one further irony—or perversity—beyond that: to allow one's spiritual powers, which ought to be redemptive, to press one further into sin:

> ... I do betray
> My nobler part to my gross body's treason;
> My soul doth tell my body that he may
> Triumph in love; flesh stays no farther reason,
> But rising at thy name doth point out thee
> As his triumphant prize; proud of this pride,
> He is contented thy poor drudge to be,
> To stand in thy affairs, fall by thy side.
>
> (151)

Not long before (in 146), the soul was urged to "Buy terms divine"; now the soul itself gives permission to the body to "Triumph in love," and this leads immediately to a sexual arousal (or "rising"). Far from triumphant, however, the poet soon becomes a "drudge"—servile, and reduced to nothing more than flesh that "stands" and "falls" according to the mistress's own desires. This servility recalls the poet's much earlier role as servant and vassal in sonnets 57–58 and elsewhere; but now, instead of resistance by the poet—in the form of irony and other modes of attack—we find complete submission.

The final poem to the mistress (152) recapitulates—in a way that is as recriminatory as it is self-accusatory—many of the implied as well as explicit experiences earlier in this group:

> In loving thee thou know'st I am forsworn,
> But thou art twice forsworn to me love swearing:
> In act thy bed-vow broke, and new faith torn
> In vowing new hate after new love bearing.
> But why of two oaths' breach do I accuse thee,
> When I break twenty? I am perjured most,
> For all my vows are oaths but to misuse thee,
> And all my honest faith in thee is lost.
> For I have sworn deep oaths of thy deep kindness,
> Oaths of thy love, thy truth, thy constancy,
> And to enlighten thee gave eyes to blindness,
> Or made them swear against the thing they see:
>> For I have sworn thee fair: more perjured eye,
>> To swear against the truth so foul a lie.
>
> (152)

The sonnet looks back to the moment when the relationship (at least for the poet) involved love, kindness, and "honest faith" sealed by oaths (lines 6–10). The mistress's infidelity was followed by a reunion ("new faith"), then betrayed once again by the dark lady: she becomes "twice forsworn."

In this recapitulation, there are obvious echoes of the sonnets addressed to the young friend, where episodes of commitment and inconstancy were central. But sonnet 152 develops this theme much further, as the poet deliberately "blinds" himself while simultaneously seeing the real nature of the mistress and his own predicament. His eyes are "perjured," but much more than perjury is involved. The poet has not only sworn "against the truth" (152), but he has consciously abandoned all reason (147), enlisted the soul itself in the pursuit of lust (151), and succumbed to a form of madness that he can anatomize and understand, but not affect:

> Th'expense of spirit in a waste of shame
> Is lust in action, and till action, lust
> Is perjured, murd'rous, bloody, full of blame,
> Savage, extreme, rude, cruel, not to trust;
> Enjoyed no sooner but despised straight,
> Past reason hunted, and no sooner had,
> Past reason hated as a swallowed bait
> On purpose laid to make the taker mad:
> Mad in pursuit and in possession so,
> Had, having, and in quest to have, extreme;
> A bliss in proof, and proved, a very woe,
> Before, a joy proposed, behind, a dream.
>> All this the world well knows yet none knows well
>> To shun the heaven that leads men to this hell.

(129)

•

Although the poet persists in his expenditure of "spirit" throughout the sonnets to the mistress, these poems are far more than a moral commentary on his actions or those of the friend. Several are as moving as any in the sequence, expressing passion, jealousy, remorse, guilt, and lust in ways that are unsurpassed. They often dramatize emotions that seem—in Yeats's phrase—wrought "to the uttermost," because Shakespeare has deliberately crystallized and given articulation to intense and torturous human feelings at their most extreme. In this sense, they recall fateful moments in Shakespearean tragedy: Othello, felled by the torments of jealousy compounded by agonizing doubt; Antony, pursued by the extravagance of his passion, even in the face of obvious abandonment; or (in the "problem plays") Angelo, surprised by sudden overpowering desire; or Troilus, confronted by Cressida's promiscuousness. Indeed, when Troilus and Cressida bid farewell to each other, he presses her to be faithful, and she questions his doubts. He replies:

> But something may be done that we will not;
> And sometimes we are devils to ourselves,
> When we will tempt the frailty of our powers,
> Presuming on their changeful potency.
>
> (IV, iv, 93–96)

The Sonnets are in one sense a testimony to the capacity of individuals to "tempt the frailty of our powers"—acting against their own wills. In *Troilus*, when the young lover is confronted with the visible proof of Cressida's unfaithfulness, he refuses to give credence to what he has witnessed. His disbelief

> doth invert th'attest of eyes and ears;
> As if those organs had deceptious functions,
> Created only to calumniate.
>
> (V, ii, 120–22)

The "deceptiveness" of one's eyes (and other senses) is clearly central to the Sonnets, and Troilus's reaction registers both belief and disbelief: "This is and is not Cressida"—a bifurcation that parallels the poet's constant incapacity to resolve the discrepancy between what he sees and what he is willing to confirm:

> So shall I live, supposing thou art true,
> Like a deceived husband; so love's face

May still seem love to me, though altered new:
Thy looks with me, thy heart in other place.

(93)

Thou blind fool, Love, what dost thou to mine eyes,
That they behold and see not what they see?

(137)

O me! what eyes hath love put in my head,
Which have no correspondence with true sight?

(148)

If the poet of the Sonnets is ultimately paralyzed in so many poems to the mistress, it is also the case that his increasing awareness of his dilemma represents a growth in self-perception. Nearly all the early sonnets to the mistress are devoted to the poet's attempt either to praise and win her or to insist upon her apparent—if not actual—devotion to him. But especially with sonnet 146 ("Poor soul, the center of my sinful earth"), he acknowledges the moral circumstances in which he finds himself. This clarity affords him no escape, but it represents an important development well beyond his earlier state. He reaches a point where he sees that:

Past cure I am, now reason is past care . . .

(147)

For thou betraying me, I do betray
My nobler part to my gross body's treason . . .

(151)

In loving thee thou know'st I am forsworn . . .
. . . I am perjured most,
For all my vows are oaths but to misuse thee,
And all my honest faith in thee is lost.

(152)

In recognizing that his reason is "past care"; that he is in the course of betraying his "nobler part"; that he is forsworn and "perjured most," the poet arrives at a new level of self-knowledge: fateful knowledge, but nonetheless a degree of awareness altogether different from his earlier deliberate self-deceptions, his lying, and his blindness in pursuit of the mistress.

Conclusion

There are several ways in which the Sonnets reveal what Richard Blackmur called a progression of "sentiments" and "almost a 'desirable' sequence with respect to the notion of development."

From the beginning, the poet plays conflicting roles, a predicament that helps to account for many of his changes in stance, tone, and subject matter as the Sonnets unfold. Because of his love for the friend—and his role as favored writer—he is committed to a poetry of praise and compliment. But as the victim of successive transgressions on the part of the young man, he expresses a range of feelings including shock, self-pity, and recrimination, while he also makes direct verbal attacks on the youth. Confronted by someone who reciprocates but also betrays love, the poet gradually becomes a questioner who seeks to discover the actual nature of his unpredictable and unfathomable friend. In the course of his journey, he reveals himself as someone doomed to doubt his own self-worth, both as a person and as a writer. He is older than the friend, less well-featured, inferior in social status, and constantly subject to feelings of self-despising: he is only too aware of his "outcast state" in a society that gives his name "a brand."

In view of the situation in which the poet finds himself (and which he partly creates), it is not surprising that the sequence should reveal many—often sudden—shifts in style and point of view, particularly in the wake of unexpected events (or in anticipation of others). These shifts do not account for all the work's frequent discontinuities (characteristic of essentially all sonnet sequences), but they do go far to explain much that might otherwise seem obscure or simply incomprehensible.

Once the nature of the poet's central predicament has been understood—that the Sonnets include incidents of expressed mutual love and successive infidelities—it becomes clear that there are a number of ways in which the sequence is ordered. There is a continual movement from an initial commitment of reciprocal affection between the poet and the friend, to a much later time when each has succumbed to (and is in the power of) the dark lady. The young man's sensual transgressions begin early in the sequence, and end with his being "enslaved" by lust. The poet is eventually unfaithful to the friend and also gives himself—with uncontrollable desire—to the mistress. In short, each of the two major figures experiences a progressive fall from an early ideal of potential mutual love, to the point where they inhabit the prison or "hell" that is in all respects "a very woe" (129). From a structural point of view, the primary focus is first on the friend's betrayals, and then on those of the poet, so that there is both a progression and a balance achieved in the work as a whole.

Another major development concerns the poet's effort to discover the true character of the young man. This involves a succession of probes, many of which follow an act of infidelity or betrayal by the youth, resulting in accusations that are increasingly serious. When the friend first abandons the poet, he is reproached and returns contrite—although the poet's reproaches are as much expressions of self-pity as they are forceful recriminations. When the young man takes possession of the poet's mistress, he receives a sharper (but ultimately contained) reaction from the poet: "Kill me with spites; yet we must not be foes" (40).

The poet's deep desire to secure the love relationship (and his role as chosen writer) clearly conflicts even more strongly with further transgressions (69–70) on the part of the friend, who is said to have grown "common," with the "rank smell of weeds." This continuous movement reaches its climax after the young man chooses a rival as his favorite. The poet ultimately characterizes the youth as a "mansion" of "vices"—a repudiation so strong that it provokes a separation and a lengthy estrangement between the two men. The youth has at last been unmasked, and seems to be fully "known." But this apparent finale proves temporary: it is followed by sonnets of self-abnegation on the part of the poet; then (in succession) a rapprochement, a celebration of recaptured love, a transgression by the poet, and—ultimately—a concluding set of powerful poems dedicated to the friend and to a new conception of love.

The poems to the mistress mirror certain aspects of the development just described. At first, the poet seems to commit himself to a novel idea of beauty—the "blackness" represented by the dark lady. Indeed, it is said (in 127) that "every tongue says beauty should look so," and the poet declares (in 131) that "Thou art the fairest and most precious jewel."

But these early expressions of admiration and love are soon qualified, and we learn (in 131) that others doubt the mistress's "power to make love groan." The poet, while disagreeing, nevertheless experiences a moment of revelation when he acknowledges that his eyes have been "corrupted" by "over-partial looks" (137). He has deceived himself, and is trapped between an irresistible desire for the mistress and an awareness that the desire is entirely at "random from the truth." His predicament is dramatized very directly in 147:

My thoughts and my discourse as madmen's are,
At random from the truth vainly expressed:
    For I have sworn thee fair, and thought thee
      bright,
Who art as black as hell, as dark as night.

(147)

This complete reversal—from an early commitment to a new ideal of "blackness" in beauty, to a recognition that the mistress is neither "fair" nor "bright"—is obviously complex, and far more aggressive than the poet's parallel moment of exclamation in sonnets 95–96. But there are clear resemblances, despite the fact that the poet and friend "recover" and are reunited, whereas the poet's slide toward uncontrolled lust for the mistress during the final poems of the entire work is single-minded and uninterrupted.

During the course of the sequence as a whole, it becomes increasingly clear that the poet is in the process of losing all that is most dear to him. First it is "Nature" who (in sonnet 20) deprives him of the young man, and in sonnet 33, the youth suddenly leaves in the company of others. The poet also "corrupts" (and loses part of) himself by excusing too readily the faults of his young friend (35)—who in turn deprives him of his mistress (40). Then a rival poet "usurps" his place (temporarily) as chosen writer. Ultimately, the youth is definitively taken from him—in thrall to the mistress: "Him have I lost, thou hast both him and me" (134). The poet (in 133) summarizes the full extent of his dispossession:

> Me from myself thy cruel eye hath taken,
> And my next self thou harder hast engrossed;
> Of him, myself, and thee I am forsaken . . .

> (133)

Throughout the course of the Sonnets, the succession of complex events gradually transforms the poet's view of Time, of beauty, of his own verse, and of the very nature of constant love. By the end, Time has become a more powerful adversary, and in the last celebratory poems to the friend, beauty ceases to play any part. Indeed, even the "eternizing" capacity of poetry itself is no longer mentioned. The poet's compounded experience—of inconstancy, of the friend's multifarious nature, and of mutability in the course of human affairs—has had a profound effect on him. His own infidelity to the young man (109–20) proves to be yet another devastating event, compelling him to accept the fact that even the strongest commitments can be disrupted by the "accidents" of Time and its ability to "Creep in 'twixt vows" and "Divert strong minds to th'course of alt'ring things" (115).

In sum, the poet is forced to question the very nature of truth in love. He concludes that it consists of the sheer power of will and determination to endure and remain constant through all life's vicissitudes, including any "alterations" or acts of infidelity, whether committed by the lover or the beloved. This recognition leads to the invigorated style—and forceful pronouncements—of sonnets 116, 121, and 123–25. Even if Death will in the end conquer all ("Our dates are brief"), the poet asserts that Time and Fortune can—during the course of life—be overcome.

THE COMPLETE SONNETS
OF WILLIAM SHAKESPEARE

SONNET I

From fairest creatures we desire increase,
That thereby beauty's rose might never die,
But as the riper should by time decease,
His tender heir might bear his memory:
But thou, contracted to thine own bright eyes,
Feed'st thy light's flame with self-substantial fuel,
Making a famine where abundance lies,
Thyself thy foe, to thy sweet self too cruel.
Thou that art now the world's fresh ornament,
And only herald to the gaudy spring,
Within thine own bud buriest thy content,
And, tender churl, mak'st waste in niggarding.
    Pity the world, or else this glutton be,
    To eat the world's due, by the grave and thee.

SONNET 2

When forty winters shall besiege thy brow,
And dig deep trenches in thy beauty's field,
Thy youth's proud livery so gazed on now
Will be a tottered weed of small worth held:
Then being asked, where all thy beauty lies,
Where all the treasure of thy lusty days,
To say within thine own deep-sunken eyes
Were an all-eating shame, and thriftless praise.
How much more praise deserved thy beauty's use,
If thou couldst answer, "This fair child of mine
Shall sum my count, and make my old excuse,"
Proving his beauty by succession thine.
    This were to be new made when thou art old,
    And see thy blood warm when thou feel'st it cold.

SONNET 3

Look in thy glass and tell the face thou viewest,
Now is the time that face should form another,
Whose fresh repair if now thou not renewest,
Thou dost beguile the world, unbless some mother.
For where is she so fair whose uneared womb
Disdains the tillage of thy husbandry?
Or who is he so fond will be the tomb
Of his self-love, to stop posterity?
Thou art thy mother's glass, and she in thee
Calls back the lovely April of her prime;
So thou through windows of thine age shalt see,
Despite of wrinkles, this thy golden time.
      But if thou live rememb'red not to be,
      Die single, and thine image dies with thee.

SONNET 4

Unthrifty loveliness, why dost thou spend
Upon thyself thy beauty's legacy?
Nature's bequest gives nothing, but doth lend,
And being frank she lends to those are free:
Then, beauteous niggard, why dost thou abuse
The bounteous largess given thee to give?
Profitless usurer, why dost thou use
So great a sum of sums yet canst not live?
For having traffic with thyself alone,
Thou of thyself thy sweet self dost deceive:
Then how when Nature calls thee to be gone,
What acceptable audit canst thou leave?
      Thy unused beauty must be tombed with thee,
      Which used lives th'executor to be.

SONNET 5

Those hours that with gentle work did frame
The lovely gaze where every eye doth dwell,
Will play the tyrants to the very same,
And that unfair which fairly doth excel:
For never-resting time leads summer on
To hideous winter and confounds him there,
Sap checked with frost and lusty leaves quite gone,
Beauty o'er-snowed and bareness every where:
Then were not summer's distillation left
A liquid prisoner pent in walls of glass,
Beauty's effect with beauty were bereft,
Nor it nor no remembrance what it was.
      But flowers distilled, though they with winter meet,
      Lose but their show; their substance still lives sweet.

SONNET 6

Then let not winter's ragged hand deface
In thee thy summer ere thou be distilled:
Make sweet some vial; treasure thou some place
With beauty's treasure ere it be self-killed:
That use is not forbidden usury
Which happies those that pay the willing loan;
That's for thyself to breed another thee,
Or ten times happier be it ten for one;
Ten times thyself were happier than thou art,
If ten of thine ten times refigured thee:
Then what could death do if thou shouldst depart,
Leaving thee living in posterity?
      Be not self-willed, for thou art much too fair
      To be death's conquest and make worms thine heir.

SONNET 7

Lo in the orient when the gracious light
Lifts up his burning head, each under-eye
Doth homage to his new-appearing sight,
Serving with looks his sacred majesty;
And having climbed the steep-up heavenly hill,
Resembling strong youth in his middle age,
Yet mortal looks adore his beauty still,
Attending on his golden pilgrimage:
But when from highmost pitch with weary car
Like feeble age he reeleth from the day,
The eyes ('fore duteous) now converted are
From his low tract and look another way:
      So thou, thyself outgoing in thy noon,
      Unlooked on diest unless thou get a son.

SONNET 8

Music to hear, why hear'st thou music sadly?
Sweets with sweets war not, joy delights in joy:
Why lov'st thou that which thou receiv'st not gladly,
Or else receiv'st with pleasure thine annoy?
If the true concord of well-tuned sounds
By unions married do offend thine ear,
They do but sweetly chide thee, who confounds
In singleness the parts that thou shouldst bear;
Mark how one string, sweet husband to another,
Strikes each in each by mutual ordering;
Resembling sire, and child, and happy mother,
Who all in one, one pleasing note do sing;
      Whose speechless song being many, seeming one,
      Sings this to thee, "Thou single wilt prove none."

SONNET 9

Is it for fear to wet a widow's eye
That thou consum'st thyself in single life?
Ah! if thou issueless shalt hap to die,
The world will wail thee like a makeless wife.
The world will be thy widow and still weep,
That thou no form of thee hast left behind,
When every private widow well may keep,
By children's eyes, her husband's shape in mind:
Look what an unthrift in the world doth spend
Shifts but his place, for still the world enjoys it;
But beauty's waste hath in the world an end,
And kept unused, the user so destroys it:
      No love toward others in that bosom sits
      That on himself such murd'rous shame commits.

SONNET 10

For shame deny that thou bear'st love to any,
Who for thy self art so unprovident.
Grant, if thou wilt, thou art beloved of many,
But that thou none lov'st is most evident;
For thou art so possessed with murd'rous hate,
That 'gainst thy self thou stick'st not to conspire,
Seeking that beauteous roof to ruinate,
Which to repair should be thy chief desire.
O change thy thought, that I may change my mind!
Shall hate be fairer lodged than gentle love?
Be as thy presence is, gracious and kind,
Or to thy self at least kind-hearted prove:
      Make thee another self for love of me,
      That beauty still may live in thine or thee.

SONNET II

As fast as thou shalt wane, so fast thou grow'st
In one of thine, from that which thou departest,
And that fresh blood which youngly thou bestow'st
Thou mayst call thine, when thou from youth convertest:
Herein lives wisdom, beauty, and increase,
Without this, folly, age, and cold decay;
If all were minded so, the times should cease,
And threescore year would make the world away.
Let those whom Nature hath not made for store,
Harsh, featureless, and rude, barrenly perish:
Look whom she best endowed she gave the more,
Which bounteous gift thou shouldst in bounty cherish.
     She carved thee for her seal, and meant thereby
     Thou shouldst print more, not let that copy die.

SONNET 12

When I do count the clock that tells the time,
And see the brave day sunk in hideous night,
When I behold the violet past prime,
And sable curls all silvered o'er with white;
When lofty trees I see barren of leaves,
Which erst from heat did canopy the herd,
And summer's green all girded up in sheaves
Borne on the bier with white and bristly beard:
Then of thy beauty do I question make
That thou among the wastes of time must go,
Since sweets and beauties do themselves forsake
And die as fast as they see others grow,
     And nothing 'gainst Time's scythe can make defence
     Save breed to brave him, when he takes thee hence.

SONNET 13

O that you were your self! but, love, you are
No longer yours than you yourself here live;
Against this coming end you should prepare,
And your sweet semblance to some other give.
So should that beauty which you hold in lease
Find no determination; then you were
Your self again after yourself's decease,
When your sweet issue your sweet form should bear.
Who lets so fair a house fall to decay,
Which husbandry in honour might uphold
Against the stormy gusts of winter's day
And barren rage of death's eternal cold?
      O none but unthrifts: dear my love, you know
      You had a father, let your son say so.

SONNET 14

Not from the stars do I my judgement pluck,
And yet methinks I have astronomy,
But not to tell of good or evil luck,
Of plagues, of dearths, or seasons' quality;
Nor can I fortune to brief minutes tell,
Pointing to each his thunder, rain, and wind,
Or say with princes if it shall go well
By oft predict that I in heaven find:
But from thine eyes my knowledge I derive,
And, constant stars, in them I read such art
As truth and beauty shall together thrive
If from thy self to store thou wouldst convert:
      Or else of thee this I prognosticate,
      Thy end is truth's and beauty's doom and date.

SONNET 15

When I consider every thing that grows
Holds in perfection but a little moment,
That this huge stage presenteth nought but shows
Whereon the stars in secret influence comment;
When I perceive that men as plants increase,
Cheered and checked even by the selfsame sky,
Vaunt in their youthful sap, at height decrease,
And wear their brave state out of memory:
Then the conceit of this inconstant stay
Sets you most rich in youth before my sight,
Where wasteful Time debateth with Decay
To change your day of youth to sullied night;
      And all in war with Time for love of you,
      As he takes from you, I engraft you new.

SONNET 16

But wherefore do not you a mightier way
Make war upon this bloody tyrant Time?
And fortify yourself in your decay
With means more blessed than my barren rhyme?
Now stand you on the top of happy hours,
And many maiden gardens, yet unset,
With virtuous wish would bear your living flowers,
Much liker than your painted counterfeit:
So should the lines of life that life repair
Which this, time's pencil, or my pupil pen
Neither in inward worth nor outward fair
Can make you live yourself in eyes of men:
      To give away yourself keeps yourself still,
      And you must live drawn by your own sweet skill.

SONNET 17

Who will believe my verse in time to come
If it were filled with your most high deserts?
Though yet, heaven knows, it is but as a tomb
Which hides your life, and shows not half your parts.
If I could write the beauty of your eyes,
And in fresh numbers number all your graces,
The age to come would say, "This poet lies;
Such heavenly touches ne'er touched earthly faces."
So should my papers (yellowed with their age)
Be scorned, like old men of less truth than tongue,
And your true rights be termed a poet's rage
And stretched meter of an antique song:

> But were some child of yours alive that time,
> You should live twice, in it and in my rhyme.

SONNET 18

Shall I compare thee to a summer's day?
Thou art more lovely and more temperate:
Rough winds do shake the darling buds of May,
And summer's lease hath all too short a date;
Sometime too hot the eye of heaven shines,
And often is his gold complexion dimmed;
And every fair from fair sometime declines,
By chance, or nature's changing course untrimmed:
But thy eternal summer shall not fade,
Nor lose possession of that fair thou ow'st,
Nor shall Death brag thou wand'rest in his shade,
When in eternal lines to time thou grow'st.

> So long as men can breathe or eyes can see,
> So long lives this, and this gives life to thee.

SONNET 19

Devouring Time, blunt thou the lion's paws,
And make the earth devour her own sweet brood,
Pluck the keen teeth from the fierce tiger's jaws,
And burn the long-lived phoenix in her blood,
Make glad and sorry seasons as thou fleet'st,
And do whate'er thou wilt, swift-footed Time,
To the wide world and all her fading sweets:
But I forbid thee one most heinous crime,
O carve not with thy hours my love's fair brow,
Nor draw no lines there with thine antique pen;
Him in thy course untainted do allow
For beauty's pattern to succeeding men.
　　　Yet do thy worst, old Time: despite thy wrong,
　　　My love shall in my verse ever live young.

SONNET 20

A woman's face with Nature's own hand painted
Hast thou, the master-mistress of my passion;
A woman's gentle heart, but not acquainted
With shifting change, as is false women's fashion;
An eye more bright than theirs, less false in rolling,
Gilding the object whereupon it gazeth;
A man in hue, all hues in his controlling,
Which steals men's eyes and women's souls amazeth.
And for a woman wert thou first created,
Till Nature as she wrought thee fell a-doting,
And by addition me of thee defeated,
By adding one thing to my purpose nothing.
　　　But since she prick'd thee out for women's pleasure,
　　　Mine be thy love, and thy love's use their treasure.

SONNET 21

So is it not with me as with that Muse
Stirred by a painted beauty to his verse,
Who heaven itself for ornament doth use,
And every fair with his fair doth rehearse,
Making a couplement of proud compare
With sun and moon, with earth and sea's rich gems,
With April's first-born flowers, and all things rare
That heaven's air in this huge rondure hems.
O let me, true in love, but truly write,
And then believe me, my love is as fair
As any mother's child, though not so bright
As those gold candles fixed in heaven's air:
  Let them say more that like of hearsay well;
  I will not praise that purpose not to sell.

SONNET 22

My glass shall not persuade me I am old,
So long as youth and thou are of one date,
But when in thee time's furrows I behold,
Then look I death my days should expiate:
For all that beauty that doth cover thee
Is but the seemly raiment of my heart,
Which in thy breast doth live, as thine in me:
How can I then be elder than thou art?
O therefore, love, be of thyself so wary
As I not for myself but for thee will,
Bearing thy heart, which I will keep so chary
As tender nurse her babe from faring ill:
  Presume not on thy heart when mine is slain;
  Thou gav'st me thine not to give back again.

SONNET 23

As an unperfect actor on the stage,
Who with his fear is put beside his part,
Or some fierce thing replete with too much rage,
Whose strength's abundance weakens his own heart;
So I, for fear of trust, forget to say
The perfect ceremony of love's rite,
And in mine own love's strength seem to decay,
O'ercharg'd with burthen of mine own love's might:
O let my books be then the eloquence
And dumb presagers of my speaking breast,
Who plead for love, and look for recompense,
More than that tongue that more hath more expressed.
   O learn to read what silent love hath writ:
   To hear with eyes belongs to love's fine wit.

SONNET 24

Mine eye hath played the painter and hath stelled
Thy beauty's form in table of my heart;
My body is the frame wherein 'tis held,
And perspective it is best painter's art.
For through the painter must you see his skill
To find where your true image pictured lies,
Which in my bosom's shop is hanging still,
That hath his windows glazed with thine eyes.
Now see what good turns eyes for eyes have done:
Mine eyes have drawn thy shape, and thine for me
Are windows to my breast, wherethrough the sun
Delights to peep, to gaze therein on thee.
   Yet eyes this cunning want to grace their art:
   They draw but what they see, know not the heart.

SONNET 25

Let those who are in favour with their stars
Of public honour and proud titles boast,
Whilst I whom fortune of such triumph bars
Unlooked for joy in that I honour most.
Great princes' favourites their fair leaves spread
But as the marigold at the sun's eye,
And in themselves their pride lies buried,
For at a frown they in their glory die.
The painful warrior famoused for fight,
After a thousand victories once foiled,
Is from the book of honour razed quite,
And all the rest forgot for which he toiled:
      Then happy I that love and am beloved
      Where I may not remove, nor be removed.

SONNET 26

Lord of my love, to whom in vassalage
Thy merit hath my duty strongly knit,
To thee I send this written ambassage
To witness duty, not to show my wit;
Duty so great, which wit so poor as mine
May make seem bare, in wanting words to show it,
But that I hope some good conceit of thine
In thy soul's thought (all naked) will bestow it,
Till whatsoever star that guides my moving
Points on me graciously with fair aspect,
And puts apparel on my tattered loving,
To show me worthy of thy sweet respect:
      Then may I dare to boast how I do love thee;
      Till then, not show my head where thou mayst prove me.

SONNET 27

Weary with toil, I haste me to my bed,
The dear repose for limbs with travel tired,
But then begins a journey in my head
To work my mind, when body's work's expired;
For then my thoughts (from far where I abide)
Intend a zealous pilgrimage to thee,
And keep my drooping eyelids open wide,
Looking on darkness which the blind do see;
Save that my soul's imaginary sight
Presents thy shadow to my sightless view,
Which like a jewel (hung in ghastly night)
Makes black night beauteous, and her old face new.
     Lo thus by day my limbs, by night my mind,
     For thee, and for myself, no quiet find.

SONNET 28

How can I then return in happy plight
That am debarred the benefit of rest?
When day's oppression is not eased by night,
But day by night and night by day oppressed;
And each (though enemies to either's reign)
Do in consent shake hands to torture me,
The one by toil, the other to complain
How far I toil, still farther off from thee.
I tell the day to please him thou art bright,
And dost him grace when clouds do blot the heaven;
So flatter I the swart-complexioned night,
When sparkling stars twire not thou gild'st the even:
     But day doth daily draw my sorrows longer,
     And night doth nightly make grief's strength seem stronger.

SONNET 29

When in disgrace with Fortune and men's eyes,
I all alone beweep my outcast state,
And trouble deaf heaven with my bootless cries,
And look upon myself and curse my fate,
Wishing me like to one more rich in hope,
Featured like him, like him with friends possessed,
Desiring this man's art, and that man's scope,
With what I most enjoy contented least;
Yet in these thoughts myself almost despising,
Haply I think on thee, and then my state
(Like to the lark at break of day arising
From sullen earth) sings hymns at heaven's gate,
  For thy sweet love rememb'red such wealth brings
  That then I scorn to change my state with kings.

SONNET 30

When to the sessions of sweet silent thought
I summon up remembrance of things past,
I sigh the lack of many a thing I sought,
And with old woes new wail my dear time's waste;
Then can I drown an eye (unused to flow)
For precious friends hid in death's dateless night,
And weep afresh love's long since cancelled woe,
And moan th'expense of many a vanished sight.
Then can I grieve at grievances foregone,
And heavily from woe to woe tell o'er
The sad account of fore-bemoaned moan,
Which I new pay as if not paid before.
  But if the while I think on thee (dear friend)
  All losses are restored, and sorrows end.

SONNET 31

Thy bosom is endeared with all hearts
Which I by lacking have supposed dead,
And there reigns love and all love's loving parts,
And all those friends which I thought buried.
How many a holy and obsequious tear
Hath dear religious love stol'n from mine eye,
As interest of the dead, which now appear
But things removed that hidden in thee lie.
Thou art the grave where buried love doth live,
Hung with the trophies of my lovers gone,
Who all their parts of me to thee did give;
That due of many, now is thine alone.
      Their images I loved, I view in thee,
      And thou (all they) hast all the all of me.

SONNET 32

If thou survive my well-contented day,
When that churl Death my bones with dust shall cover,
And shalt by fortune once more re-survey
These poor rude lines of thy deceased lover,
Compare them with the bett'ring of the time,
And though they be outstripped by every pen,
Reserve them for my love, not for their rhyme,
Exceeded by the height of happier men.
O then vouchsafe me but this loving thought:
"Had my friend's Muse grown with this growing age,
A dearer birth than this his love had brought,
To march in ranks of better equipage:
      But since he died and poets better prove,
      Theirs for their style I'll read, his for his love."

SONNET 33

Full many a glorious morning have I seen
Flatter the mountain tops with sovereign eye,
Kissing with golden face the meadows green,
Gilding pale streams with heavenly alchemy;
Anon permit the basest clouds to ride
With ugly rack on his celestial face,
And from the forlorn world his visage hide,
Stealing unseen to west with this disgrace:
Even so my sun one early morn did shine
With all triumphant splendour on my brow;
But out alack, he was but one hour mine,
The region cloud hath masked him from me now.
      Yet him for this my love no whit disdaineth:
      Suns of the world may stain, when heaven's sun staineth.

SONNET 34

Why didst thou promise such a beauteous day,
And make me travel forth without my cloak,
To let base clouds o'ertake me in my way,
Hiding thy brav'ry in their rotten smoke?
'Tis not enough that through the cloud thou break,
To dry the rain on my storm-beaten face,
For no man well of such a salve can speak,
That heals the wound, and cures not the disgrace:
Nor can thy shame give physic to my grief;
Though thou repent, yet I have still the loss:
Th'offender's sorrow lends but weak relief
To him that bears the strong offence's cross.
      Ah, but those tears are pearl which thy love sheeds,
      And they are rich, and ransom all ill deeds.

SONNET 35

No more be grieved at that which thou hast done:
Roses have thorns, and silver fountains mud,
Clouds and eclipses stain both moon and sun,
And loathsome canker lives in sweetest bud.
All men make faults, and even I in this,
Authorising thy trespass with compare,
My self corrupting salving thy amiss,
Excusing thy sins more than their sins are;
For to thy sensual fault I bring in sense—
Thy adverse party is thy advocate—
And 'gainst myself a lawful plea commence:
Such civil war is in my love and hate
      That I an accessory needs must be
      To that sweet thief which sourly robs from me.

SONNET 36

Let me confess that we two must be twain,
Although our undivided loves are one:
So shall those blots that do with me remain,
Without thy help, by me be borne alone.
In our two loves there is but one respect,
Though in our lives a separable spite,
Which though it alter not love's sole effect,
Yet doth it steal sweet hours from love's delight.
I may not evermore acknowledge thee,
Lest my bewailed guilt should do thee shame,
Nor thou with public kindness honour me,
Unless thou take that honour from thy name:
      But do not so; I love thee in such sort,
      As thou being mine, mine is thy good report.

SONNET 37

As a decrepit father takes delight
To see his active child do deeds of youth,
So I, made lame by Fortune's dearest spite,
Take all my comfort of thy worth and truth;
For whether beauty, birth, or wealth, or wit,
Or any of these all, or all, or more,
Entitled in thy parts do crowned sit,
I make my love engrafted to this store:
So then I am not lame, poor, nor despised,
Whilst that this shadow doth such substance give
That I in thy abundance am sufficed,
And by a part of all thy glory live.
　　　　Look what is best, that best I wish in thee;
　　　　This wish I have, then ten times happy me.

SONNET 38

How can my Muse want subject to invent
While thou dost breathe, that pour'st into my verse
Thine own sweet argument, too excellent
For every vulgar paper to rehearse?
O give thyself the thanks if aught in me
Worthy perusal stand against thy sight,
For who's so dumb that cannot write to thee,
When thou thyself dost give invention light?
Be thou the tenth Muse, ten times more in worth
Than those old nine which rhymers invocate;
And he that calls on thee, let him bring forth
Eternal numbers to outlive long date.
　　　　If my slight Muse do please these curious days,
　　　　The pain be mine, but thine shall be the praise.

SONNET 39

O how thy worth with manners may I sing,
When thou art all the better part of me?
What can mine own praise to mine own self bring,
And what is't but mine own when I praise thee?
Even for this, let us divided live,
And our dear love lose name of single one,
That by this separation I may give
That due to thee which thou deserv'st alone.
O absence, what a torment wouldst thou prove,
Were it not thy sour leisure gave sweet leave
To entertain the time with thoughts of love,
Which time and thoughts so sweetly dost deceive;
   And that thou teachest how to make one twain,
   By praising him here who doth hence remain.

SONNET 40

Take all my loves, my love, yea take them all;
What hast thou then more than thou hadst before?
No love, my love, that thou mayst true love call,
All mine was thine, before thou hadst this more.
Then if for my love thou my love receivest,
I cannot blame thee, for my love thou usest;
But yet be blamed, if thou this self deceivest
By wilful taste of what thyself refusest.
I do forgive thy robb'ry, gentle thief,
Although thou steal thee all my poverty;
And yet love knows it is a greater grief
To bear love's wrong than hate's known injury.
   Lascivious grace, in whom all ill well shows,
   Kill me with spites; yet we must not be foes.

SONNET 41

Those pretty wrongs that liberty commits
When I am sometime absent from thy heart,
Thy beauty, and thy years, full well befits,
For still temptation follows where thou art.
Gentle thou art, and therefore to be won,
Beauteous thou art, therefore to be assailed;
And when a woman woos, what woman's son
Will sourly leave her till she have prevailed?
Ay me, but yet thou mightst my seat forbear,
And chide thy beauty, and thy straying youth,
Who lead thee in their riot even there
Where thou art forced to break a twofold truth:
       Hers, by thy beauty tempting her to thee,
       Thine, by thy beauty being false to me.

SONNET 42

That thou hast her, it is not all my grief,
And yet it may be said I loved her dearly;
That she hath thee is of my wailing chief,
A loss in love that touches me more nearly.
Loving offenders, thus I will excuse ye:
Thou dost love her because thou know'st I love her,
And for my sake even so doth she abuse me,
Suff'ring my friend for my sake to approve her.
If I lose thee, my loss is my love's gain,
And losing her, my friend hath found that loss,
Both find each other, and I lose both twain,
And both for my sake lay on me this cross.
       But here's the joy, my friend and I are one:
       Sweet flattery! then she loves but me alone.

SONNET 43

When most I wink then do mine eyes best see,
For all the day they view things unrespected,
But when I sleep, in dreams they look on thee,
And darkly bright, are bright in dark directed.
Then thou, whose shadow shadows doth make bright,
How would thy shadow's form form happy show
To the clear day with thy much clearer light,
When to unseeing eyes thy shade shines so!
How would (I say) mine eyes be blessed made,
By looking on thee in the living day,
When in dead night thy fair imperfect shade
Through heavy sleep on sightless eyes doth stay!
  All days are nights to see till I see thee,
  And nights bright days when dreams do show thee me.

SONNET 44

If the dull substance of my flesh were thought,
Injurious distance should not stop my way,
For then despite of space I would be brought,
From limits far remote, where thou dost stay.
No matter then although my foot did stand
Upon the farthest earth removed from thee,
For nimble thought can jump both sea and land
As soon as think the place where he would be.
But ah, thought kills me that I am not thought,
To leap large lengths of miles when thou art gone,
But that, so much of earth and water wrought,
I must attend time's leisure with my moan,
  Receiving naught by elements so slow
  But heavy tears, badges of either's woe.

SONNET 45

The other two, slight air and purging fire,
Are both with thee, wherever I abide;
The first my thought, the other my desire,
These present-absent with swift motion slide.
For when these quicker elements are gone
In tender embassy of love to thee,
My life, being made of four, with two alone
Sinks down to death, oppressed with melancholy,
Until life's composition be recured
By those swift messengers returned from thee,
Who even but now come back again assured
Of thy fair health, recounting it to me.
   This told, I joy, but then no longer glad,
   I send them back again and straight grow sad.

SONNET 46

Mine eye and heart are at a mortal war,
How to divide the conquest of thy sight.
Mine eye my heart thy picture's sight would bar,
My heart mine eye the freedom of that right.
My heart doth plead that thou in him dost lie
(A closet never pierced with crystal eyes),
But the defendant doth that plea deny,
And says in him thy fair appearance lies.
To 'cide this title is impannelled
A quest of thoughts, all tenants to the heart,
And by their verdict is determined
The clear eye's moiety, and the dear heart's part,
   As thus: mine eye's due is thy outward part,
   And my heart's right thy inward love of heart.

SONNET 47

Betwixt mine eye and heart a league is took,
And each doth good turns now unto the other:
When that mine eye is famished for a look,
Or heart in love with sighs himself doth smother,
With my love's picture then my eye doth feast,
And to the painted banquet bids my heart;
Another time mine eye is my heart's guest,
And in his thoughts of love doth share a part.
So either by thy picture or my love,
Thyself, away, are present still with me,
For thou not farther than my thoughts canst move,
And I am still with them, and they with thee;
      Or if they sleep, thy picture in my sight
      Awakes my heart to heart's and eye's delight.

SONNET 48

How careful was I, when I took my way,
Each trifle under truest bars to thrust,
That to my use it might unused stay
From hands of falsehood, in sure wards of trust!
But thou, to whom my jewels trifles are,
Most worthy comfort, now my greatest grief,
Thou best of dearest, and mine only care,
Art left the prey of every vulgar thief.
Thee have I not locked up in any chest,
Save where thou art not, though I feel thou art,
Within the gentle closure of my breast,
From whence at pleasure thou mayst come and part;
      And even thence thou wilt be stol'n, I fear,
      For truth proves thievish for a prize so dear.

SONNET 49

Against that time (if ever that time come)
When I shall see thee frown on my defects,
Whenas thy love hath cast his utmost sum,
Called to that audit by advised respects;
Against that time when thou shalt strangely pass,
And scarcely greet me with that sun, thine eye,
When love converted from the thing it was
Shall reasons find of settled gravity:
Against that time do I ensconce me here
Within the knowledge of mine own desert,
And this my hand against myself uprear,
To guard the lawful reasons on thy part:
     To leave poor me thou hast the strength of laws,
     Since why to love I can allege no cause.

SONNET 50

How heavy do I journey on the way,
When what I seek (my weary travel's end)
Doth teach that ease and that repose to say
"Thus far the miles are measured from thy friend."
The beast that bears me, tired with my woe,
Plods dully on, to bear that weight in me,
As if by some instinct the wretch did know
His rider loved not speed being made from thee:
The bloody spur cannot provoke him on,
That sometimes anger thrusts into his hide,
Which heavily he answers with a groan,
More sharp to me than spurring to his side;
     For that same groan doth put this in my mind:
     My grief lies onward and my joy behind.

SONNET 51

Thus can my love excuse the slow offence
Of my dull bearer, when from thee I speed:
From where thou art, why should I haste me thence?
Till I return, of posting is no need.
O what excuse will my poor beast then find,
When swift extremity can seem but slow?
Then should I spur, though mounted on the wind,
In winged speed no motion shall I know:
Then can no horse with my desire keep pace;
Therefore desire (of perfect'st love being made)
Shall weigh no dull flesh in his fiery race,
But love, for love, thus shall excuse my jade:
  Since from thee going he went willful slow,
  Towards thee I'll run, and give him leave to go.

SONNET 52

So am I as the rich whose blessed key
Can bring him to his sweet up-locked treasure,
The which he will not ev'ry hour survey,
For blunting the fine point of seldom pleasure.
Therefore are feasts so solemn and so rare,
Since, seldom coming, in the long year set,
Like stones of worth they thinly placed are,
Or captain jewels in the carcanet.
So is the time that keeps you as my chest,
Or as the ward-robe which the robe doth hide,
To make some special instant special blest,
By new unfolding his imprisoned pride.
  Blessed are you whose worthiness gives scope,
  Being had to triumph, being lacked, to hope.

SONNET 53

What is your substance, whereof are you made,
That millions of strange shadows on you tend?
Since every one hath, every one, one shade,
And you, but one, can every shadow lend.
Describe Adonis, and the counterfeit
Is poorly imitated after you;
On Helen's cheek all art of beauty set,
And you in Grecian tires are painted new;
Speak of the spring and foison of the year,
The one doth shadow of your beauty show,
The other as your bounty doth appear,
And you in every blessed shape we know.
>   In all external grace you have some part,
>   But you like none, none you, for constant heart.

SONNET 54

O how much more doth beauty beauteous seem
By that sweet ornament which truth doth give!
The rose looks fair, but fairer we it deem
For that sweet odour which doth in it live.
The canker blooms have full as deep a dye
As the perfumed tincture of the roses,
Hang on such thorns, and play as wantonly,
When summer's breath their masked buds discloses;
But for their virtue only is their show,
They live unwooed, and unrespected fade,
Die to themselves. Sweet roses do not so,
Of their sweet deaths are sweetest odours made:
>   And so of you, beauteous and lovely youth,
>   When that shall vade, my verse distills your truth.

SONNET 55

Not marble nor the gilded monuments
Of princes shall outlive this pow'rful rhyme,
But you shall shine more bright in these contents
Than unswept stone, besmeared with sluttish time.
When wasteful war shall statues overturn,
And broils root out the work of masonry,
Nor Mars his sword, nor war's quick fire shall burn
The living record of your memory.
'Gainst death and all oblivious enmity
Shall you pace forth; your praise shall still find room
Even in the eyes of all posterity
That wear this world out to the ending doom.
      So, till the judgement that your self arise,
      You live in this, and dwell in lovers' eyes.

SONNET 56

Sweet love, renew thy force, be it not said
Thy edge should blunter be than appetite,
Which but today by feeding is allayed,
Tomorrow sharpened in his former might.
So, love, be thou: although today thou fill
Thy hungry eyes even till they wink with fullness,
Tomorrow see again, and do not kill
The spirit of love with a perpetual dullness:
Let this sad int'rim like the ocean be,
Which parts the shore, where two contracted new
Come daily to the banks, that when they see
Return of love, more blest may be the view;
      As call it winter, which being full of care,
      Makes summer's welcome, thrice more wished, more rare.

SONNET 57

Being your slave, what should I do but tend
Upon the hours and times of your desire?
I have no precious time at all to spend,
Nor services to do till you require.
Nor dare I chide the world-without-end hour
Whilst I (my sovereign) watch the clock for you,
Nor think the bitterness of absence sour
When you have bid your servant once adieu.
Nor dare I question with my jealous thought
Where you may be, or your affairs suppose,
But like a sad slave stay and think of nought
Save where you are how happy you make those.
      So true a fool is love that in your will
      (Though you do any thing) he thinks no ill.

SONNET 58

That god forbid, that made me first your slave,
I should in thought control your times of pleasure,
Or at your hand th'account of hours to crave,
Being your vassal bound to stay your leisure.
O let me suffer (being at your beck)
Th'imprisoned absence of your liberty,
And patience, tame to sufferance, bide each check,
Without accusing you of injury.
Be where you list, your charter is so strong
That you yourself may privilege your time
To what you will; to you it doth belong
Yourself to pardon of self-doing crime.
      I am to wait, though waiting so be hell,
      Not blame your pleasure, be it ill or well.

SONNET 59

If there be nothing new, but that which is
Hath been before, how are our brains beguiled,
Which, labouring for invention, bear amiss
The second burthen of a former child!
O that record could with a backward look,
Even of five hundred courses of the sun,
Show me your image in some antique book,
Since mind at first in character was done,
That I might see what the old world could say
To this composed wonder of your frame:
Whether we are mended, or whe'er better they,
Or whether revolution be the same.
      O sure I am the wits of former days
      To subjects worse have given admiring praise.

SONNET 60

Like as the waves make towards the pebbled shore,
So do our minutes hasten to their end,
Each changing place with that which goes before,
In sequent toil all forwards do contend.
Nativity, once in the main of light,
Crawls to maturity, wherewith being crowned,
Crooked eclipses 'gainst his glory fight,
And Time that gave doth now his gift confound.
Time doth transfix the flourish set on youth,
And delves the parallels in beauty's brow,
Feeds on the rarities of nature's truth,
And nothing stands but for his scythe to mow.
      And yet to times in hope my verse shall stand
      Praising thy worth, despite his cruel hand.

SONNET 61

Is it thy will thy image should keep open
My heavy eyelids to the weary night?
Dost thou desire my slumbers should be broken,
While shadows like to thee do mock my sight?
Is it thy spirit that thou send'st from thee
So far from home into my deeds to pry,
To find out shames and idle hours in me,
The scope and tenor of thy jealousy?
O no, thy love, though much, is not so great;
It is my love that keeps mine eye awake,
Mine own true love that doth my rest defeat,
To play the watchman ever for thy sake.
    For thee watch I, whilst thou dost wake elsewhere,
    From me far off, with others all too near.

SONNET 62

Sin of self-love possesseth all mine eye,
And all my soul, and all my every part;
And for this sin there is no remedy,
It is so grounded inward in my heart.
Methinks no face so gracious is as mine,
No shape so true, no truth of such account,
And for myself mine own worth do define,
As I all other in all worths surmount.
But when my glass shows me myself indeed,
Beated and chopped with tanned antiquity,
Mine own self-love quite contrary I read;
Self so self-loving were iniquity.
    'Tis thee (my self) that for myself I praise,
    Painting my age with beauty of thy days.

SONNET 63

Against my love shall be as I am now,
With Time's injurious hand crushed and o'er-worn,
When hours have drained his blood and filled his brow
With lines and wrinkles, when his youthful morn
Hath travelled on to Age's steepy night,
And all those beauties whereof now he's king
Are vanishing, or vanished out of sight,
Stealing away the treasure of his spring:
For such a time do I now fortify
Against confounding Age's cruel knife,
That he shall never cut from memory
My sweet love's beauty, though my lover's life.
      His beauty shall in these black lines be seen,
      And they shall live, and he in them still green.

SONNET 64

When I have seen by Time's fell hand defaced
The rich proud cost of outworn buried age,
When sometime lofty towers I see down razed,
And brass eternal slave to mortal rage;
When I have seen the hungry ocean gain
Advantage on the kingdom of the shore,
And the firm soil win of the wat'ry main,
Increasing store with loss, and loss with store;
When I have seen such interchange of state,
Or state itself confounded to decay,
Ruin hath taught me thus to ruminate,
That Time will come and take my love away.
      This thought is as a death, which cannot choose
      But weep to have that which it fears to lose.

SONNET 65

Since brass, nor stone, nor earth, nor boundless sea,
But sad mortality o'er-sways their power,
How with this rage shall beauty hold a plea,
Whose action is no stronger than a flower?
O how shall summer's honey breath hold out
Against the wrackful siege of batt'ring days,
When rocks impregnable are not so stout,
Nor gates of steel so strong, but Time decays?
O fearful meditation: Where, alack,
Shall Time's best jewel from Time's chest lie hid?
Or what strong hand can hold his swift foot back?
Or who his spoil of beauty can forbid?
      O none, unless this miracle have might,
      That in black ink my love may still shine bright.

SONNET 66

Tired with all these, for restful death I cry:
As to behold desert a beggar born,
And needy nothing trimmed in jollity,
And purest faith unhappily forsworn,
And gilded honour shamefully misplaced,
And maiden virtue rudely strumpeted,
And right perfection wrongfully disgraced,
And strength by limping sway disabled,
And art made tongue-tied by authority,
And folly (doctor-like) controlling skill,
And simple truth miscalled simplicity,
And captive good attending captain ill.
      Tired with all these, from these would I be gone,
      Save that to die, I leave my love alone.

SONNET 67

Ah wherefore with infection should he live,
And with his presence grace impiety,
That sin by him advantage should achieve,
And lace itself with his society?
Why should false painting imitate his cheek,
And steal dead seeing of his living hue?
Why should poor beauty indirectly seek
Roses of shadow, since his rose is true?
Why should he live, now Nature bankrupt is,
Beggared of blood to blush through lively veins,
For she hath no exchequer now but his,
And proud of many, lives upon his gains?
      O him she stores, to show what wealth she had
      In days long since, before these last so bad.

SONNET 68

Thus is his cheek the map of days outworn,
When beauty lived and died as flowers do now,
Before the bastard signs of fair were borne,
Or durst inhabit on a living brow;
Before the golden tresses of the dead,
The right of sepulchres, were shorn away,
To live a second life on second head,
Ere beauty's dead fleece made another gay:
In him those holy antique hours are seen
Without all ornament, itself and true,
Making no summer of another's green,
Robbing no old to dress his beauty new;
      And him as for a map doth Nature store,
      To show false Art what beauty was of yore.

SONNET 69

Those parts of thee that the world's eye doth view
Want nothing that the thought of hearts can mend;
All tongues (the voice of souls) give thee that due,
Utt'ring bare truth, even so as foes commend.
Thy outward thus with outward praise is crowned,
But those same tongues that give thee so thine own,
In other accents do this praise confound
By seeing farther than the eye hath shown.
They look into the beauty of thy mind,
And that in guess they measure by thy deeds;
Then, churls, their thoughts (although their eyes were kind)
To thy fair flower add the rank smell of weeds:
  But why thy odour matcheth not thy show,
  The soil is this, that thou dost common grow.

SONNET 70

That thou are blamed shall not be thy defect,
For slander's mark was ever yet the fair;
The ornament of beauty is suspect,
A crow that flies in heaven's sweetest air.
So thou be good, slander doth but approve
Thy worth the greater, being wooed of time,
For canker vice the sweetest buds doth love,
And thou present'st a pure unstained prime.
Thou hast passed by the ambush of young days,
Either not assailed, or victor, being charged;
Yet this thy praise cannot be so thy praise
To tie up envy, evermore enlarged:
  If some suspect of ill masked not thy show,
  Then thou alone kingdoms of hearts shouldst owe.

SONNET 71

No longer mourn for me when I am dead
Than you shall hear the surly sullen bell
Give warning to the world that I am fled,
From this vile world with vilest worms to dwell;
Nay, if you read this line, remember not
The hand that writ it, for I love you so,
That I in your sweet thoughts would be forgot,
If thinking on me then should make you woe.
O if (I say) you look upon this verse,
When I (perhaps) compounded am with clay,
Do not so much as my poor name rehearse,
But let your love even with my life decay,
    Lest the wise world should look into your moan,
    And mock you with me after I am gone.

SONNET 72

O lest the world should task you to recite
What merit lived in me that you should love,
After my death (dear love) forget me quite,
For you in me can nothing worthy prove;
Unless you would devise some virtuous lie
To do more for me than mine own desert,
And hang more praise upon deceased I
Than niggard truth would willingly impart:
O lest your true love may seem false in this,
That you for love speak well of me untrue,
My name be buried where my body is,
And live no more to shame nor me nor you:
    For I am shamed by that which I bring forth,
    And so should you, to love things nothing worth.

SONNET 73

That time of year thou mayst in me behold
When yellow leaves, or none, or few, do hang
Upon those boughs which shake against the cold,
Bare ruined choirs, where late the sweet birds sang.
In me thou seest the twilight of such day
As after sunset fadeth in the west,
Which by and by black night doth take away,
Death's second self that seals up all in rest.
In me thou seest the glowing of such fire
That on the ashes of his youth doth lie,
As the death-bed whereon it must expire,
Consumed with that which it was nourished by.
     This thou perceiv'st, which makes thy love more strong,
     To love that well which thou must leave ere long.

SONNET 74

But be contented when that fell arrest
Without all bail shall carry me away,
My life hath in this line some interest,
Which for memorial still with thee shall stay.
When thou reviewest this, thou dost review
The very part was consecrate to thee:
The earth can have but earth, which is his due;
My spirit is thine, the better part of me.
So then thou hast but lost the dregs of life,
The prey of worms, my body being dead,
The coward conquest of a wretch's knife,
Too base of thee to be remembered:
     The worth of that is that which it contains,
     And that is this, and this with thee remains.

SONNET 75

So are you to my thoughts as food to life,
Or as sweet seasoned showers are to the ground;
And for the peace of you I hold such strife
As 'twixt a miser and his wealth is found:
Now proud as an enjoyer, and anon
Doubting the filching age will steal his treasure;
Now counting best to be with you alone,
Then bettered that the world may see my pleasure;
Sometime all full with feasting on your sight,
And by and by clean starved for a look;
Possessing or pursuing no delight
Save what is had, or must from you be took.
> Thus do I pine and surfeit day by day,
> Or gluttoning on all, or all away.

SONNET 76

Why is my verse so barren of new pride?
So far from variation or quick change?
Why with the time do I not glance aside
To new-found methods and to compounds strange?
Why write I still all one, ever the same,
And keep invention in a noted weed,
That every word doth almost tell my name,
Showing their birth, and where they did proceed?
O know, sweet love, I always write of you,
And you and love are still my argument;
So all my best is dressing old words new,
Spending again what is already spent:
> For as the sun is daily new and old,
> So is my love still telling what is told.

SONNET 77

Thy glass will show thee how thy beauties wear,
Thy dial how thy precious minutes waste;
The vacant leaves thy mind's imprint will bear,
And of this book, this learning mayst thou taste:
The wrinkles which thy glass will truly show
Of mouthed graves will give thee memory,
Thou by thy dial's shady stealth mayst know
Time's thievish progress to eternity.
Look what thy memory cannot contain
Commit to these waste blanks, and thou shalt find
Those children nursed, delivered from thy brain,
To take a new acquaintance of thy mind.
      These offices, so oft as thou wilt look,
      Shall profit thee, and much enrich thy book.

SONNET 78

So oft have I invoked thee for my Muse,
And found such fair assistance in my verse,
As every alien pen hath got my use,
And under thee their poesy disperse.
Thine eyes, that taught the dumb on high to sing,
And heavy ignorance aloft to fly,
Have added feathers to the learned's wing,
And given grace a double majesty.
Yet be most proud of that which I compile,
Whose influence is thine, and born of thee:
In others' works thou dost but mend the style,
And arts with thy sweet graces graced be;
      But thou art all my art, and dost advance
      As high as learning my rude ignorance.

SONNET 79

Whilst I alone did call upon thy aid,
My verse alone had all thy gentle grace,
But now my gracious numbers are decayed,
And my sick Muse doth give another place.
I grant (sweet love) thy lovely argument
Deserves the travail of a worthier pen,
Yet what of thee thy poet doth invent
He robs thee of, and pays it thee again:
He lends thee virtue, and he stole that word
From thy behaviour; beauty doth he give,
And found it in thy cheek; he can afford
No praise to thee but what in thee doth live.
　　　　Then thank him not for that which he doth say,
　　　　Since what he owes thee, thou thyself dost pay.

SONNET 80

O how I faint when I of you do write,
Knowing a better spirit doth use your name,
And in the praise thereof spends all his might,
To make me tongue-tied speaking of your fame.
But since your worth (wide as the ocean is)
The humble as the proudest sail doth bear,
My saucy bark (inferior far to his)
On your broad main doth wilfully appear.
Your shallowest help will hold me up afloat,
Whilst he upon your soundless deep doth ride,
Or (being wracked) I am a worthless boat,
He of tall building and of goodly pride.
　　　　Then if he thrive and I be cast away,
　　　　The worst was this: my love was my decay.

SONNET 81

Or I shall live your epitaph to make,
Or you survive when I in earth am rotten,
From hence your memory death cannot take,
Although in me each part will be forgotten.
Your name from hence immortal life shall have,
Though I (once gone) to all the world must die;
The earth can yield me but a common grave,
When you entombed in men's eyes shall lie:
Your monument shall be my gentle verse,
Which eyes not yet created shall o'er-read,
And tongues to be your being shall rehearse,
When all the breathers of this world are dead;
     You still shall live (such virtue hath my pen)
     Where breath most breathes, even in the mouths of men.

SONNET 82

I grant thou wert not married to my Muse,
And therefore mayst without attaint o'erlook
The dedicated words which writers use
Of their fair subject, blessing every book.
Thou art as fair in knowledge as in hue,
Finding thy worth a limit past my praise,
And therefore art enforced to seek anew
Some fresher stamp of the time-bettering days.
And do so, love; yet when they have devised
What strained touches rhetoric can lend,
Thou, truly fair, wert truly sympathised
In true plain words by thy true-telling friend;
     And their gross painting might be better used
     Where cheeks need blood; in thee it is abused.

SONNET 83

I never saw that you did painting need,
And therefore to your fair no painting set;
I found (or thought I found) you did exceed
The barren tender of a poet's debt:
And therefore have I slept in your report,
That you yourself being extant well might show
How far a modern quill doth come too short,
Speaking of worth, what worth in you doth grow.
This silence for my sin you did impute,
Which shall be most my glory, being dumb;
For I impair not beauty, being mute,
When others would give life, and bring a tomb.
      There lives more life in one of your fair eyes
      Than both your poets can in praise devise.

SONNET 84

Who is it that says most which can say more
Than this rich praise: that you alone are you,
In whose confine immured is the store
Which should example where your equal grew?
Lean penury within that pen doth dwell,
That to his subject lends not some small glory,
But he that writes of you, if he can tell
That you are you, so dignifies his story.
Let him but copy what in you is writ,
Not making worse what nature made so clear,
And such a counterpart shall fame his wit,
Making his style admired everywhere.
      You to your beauteous blessings add a curse,
      Being fond on praise, which makes your praises worse.

SONNET 85

My tongue-tied Muse in manners holds her still,
While comments of your praise, richly compiled,
Reserve their character with golden quill
And precious phrase by all the Muses filed.
I think good thoughts, whilst others write good words,
And like unlettered clerk still cry "Amen"
To every hymn that able spirit affords
In polished form of well-refined pen.
Hearing you praised, I say, " 'Tis so, 'tis true,"
And to the most of praise add something more;
But that is in my thought, whose love to you
(Though words come hindmost) holds his rank before.
      Then others for the breath of words respect,
      Me for my dumb thoughts, speaking in effect.

SONNET 86

Was it the proud full sail of his great verse,
Bound for the prize of (all too precious) you,
That did my ripe thoughts in my brain inhearse,
Making their tomb the womb wherein they grew?
Was it his spirit, by spirits taught to write
Above a mortal pitch, that struck me dead?
No, neither he, nor his compeers by night
Giving him aid, my verse astonished.
He, nor that affable familiar ghost
Which nightly gulls him with intelligence,
As victors of my silence cannot boast;
I was not sick of any fear from thence.
      But when your countenance filled up his line,
      Then lacked I matter, that enfeebled mine.

SONNET 87

Farewell, thou art too dear for my possessing,
And like enough thou know'st thy estimate;
The charter of thy worth gives thee releasing:
My bonds in thee are all determinate.
For how do I hold thee but by thy granting?
And for that riches where is my deserving?
The cause of this fair gift in me is wanting,
And so my patent back again is swerving.
Thy self thou gav'st, thy own worth then not knowing,
Or me, to whom thou gav'st it, else mistaking;
So thy great gift, upon misprision growing,
Comes home again, on better judgement making.
    Thus have I had thee as a dream doth flatter,
    In sleep a king, but waking no such matter.

SONNET 88

When thou shalt be disposed to set me light,
And place my merit in the eye of scorn,
Upon thy side against myself I'll fight,
And prove thee virtuous, though thou art forsworn:
With mine own weakness being best acquainted,
Upon thy part I can set down a story
Of faults concealed wherein I am attainted,
That thou in losing me shall win much glory;
And I by this will be a gainer too,
For, bending all my loving thoughts on thee,
The injuries that to myself I do,
Doing thee vantage, double vantage me.
    Such is my love, to thee I so belong,
    That for thy right myself will bear all wrong.

SONNET 89

Say that thou didst forsake me for some fault,
And I will comment upon that offence;
Speak of my lameness, and I straight will halt,
Against thy reasons making no defence.
Thou canst not (love) disgrace me half so ill,
To set a form upon desired change,
As I'll myself disgrace; knowing thy will,
I will acquaintance strangle and look strange,
Be absent from thy walks, and in my tongue
Thy sweet beloved name no more shall dwell,
Lest I (too much profane) should do it wrong,
And haply of our old acquaintance tell.
       For thee, against myself I'll vow debate,
       For I must ne'er love him whom thou dost hate.

SONNET 90

Then hate me when thou wilt, if ever, now,
Now while the world is bent my deeds to cross,
Join with the spite of Fortune, make me bow,
And do not drop in for an after-loss.
Ah do not, when my heart hath scaped this sorrow,
Come in the rearward of a conquered woe;
Give not a windy night a rainy morrow,
To linger out a purposed overthrow.
If thou wilt leave me, do not leave me last,
When other petty griefs have done their spite,
But in the onset come; so shall I taste
At first the very worst of Fortune's might;
       And other strains of woe, which now seem woe,
       Compared with loss of thee, will not seem so.

SONNET 91

Some glory in their birth, some in their skill,
Some in their wealth, some in their body's force,
Some in their garments, though newfangled ill,
Some in their hawks and hounds, some in their horse;
And every humour hath his adjunct pleasure,
Wherein it finds a joy above the rest;
But these particulars are not my measure,
All these I better in one general best.
Thy love is better than high birth to me,
Richer than wealth, prouder than garments' cost,
Of more delight than hawks and horses be;
And having thee, of all men's pride I boast:
   Wretched in this alone, that thou mayst take
   All this away, and me most wretched make.

SONNET 92

But do thy worst to steal thyself away,
For term of life thou art assured mine,
And life no longer than thy love will stay,
For it depends upon that love of thine.
Then need I not to fear the worst of wrongs,
When in the least of them my life hath end;
I see a better state of me belongs
Than that which on thy humour doth depend.
Thou canst not vex me with inconstant mind,
Since that my life on thy revolt doth lie.
O what a happy title do I find,
Happy to have thy love, happy to die!
   But what's so blessed-fair that fears no blot?
   Thou mayst be false, and yet I know it not.

SONNET 93

So shall I live, supposing thou art true,
Like a deceived husband; so love's face
May still seem love to me, though altered new:
Thy looks with me, thy heart in other place.
For there can live no hatred in thine eye,
Therefore in that I cannot know thy change;
In many's looks, the false heart's history
Is writ in moods and frowns and wrinkles strange,
But heaven in thy creation did decree
That in thy face sweet love should ever dwell;
Whate'er thy thoughts or thy heart's workings be,
Thy looks should nothing thence but sweetness tell.
      How like Eve's apple doth thy beauty grow,
      If thy sweet virtue answer not thy show!

SONNET 94

They that have pow'r to hurt, and will do none,
That do not do the thing they most do show,
Who, moving others, are themselves as stone,
Unmoved, cold, and to temptation slow—
They rightly do inherit heaven's graces,
And husband nature's riches from expense;
They are the lords and owners of their faces,
Others but stewards of their excellence.
The summer's flow'r is to the summer sweet,
Though to itself it only live and die,
But if that flow'r with base infection meet,
The basest weed outbraves his dignity:
      For sweetest things turn sourest by their deeds;
      Lilies that fester smell far worse than weeds.

SONNET 95

How sweet and lovely dost thou make the shame
Which, like a canker in the fragrant rose,
Doth spot the beauty of thy budding name!
O, in what sweets dost thou thy sins enclose!
That tongue that tells the story of thy days
(Making lascivious comments on thy sport)
Cannot dispraise but in a kind of praise,
Naming thy name blesses an ill report.
O, what a mansion have those vices got
Which for their habitation chose out thee,
Where beauty's veil doth cover every blot,
And all things turns to fair that eyes can see!
      Take heed (dear heart) of this large privilege:
      The hardest knife ill-used doth lose his edge.

SONNET 96

Some say thy fault is youth, some wantonness,
Some say thy grace is youth and gentle sport;
Both grace and faults are loved of more and less:
Thou mak'st faults graces that to thee resort.
As on the finger of a throned queen
The basest jewel will be well esteemed,
So are those errors that in thee are seen
To truths translated, and for true things deemed.
How many lambs might the stern wolf betray,
If like a lamb he could his looks translate!
How many gazers mightst thou lead away,
If thou wouldst use the strength of all thy state!
      But do not so; I love thee in such sort,
      As thou being mine, mine is thy good report.

SONNET 97

How like a winter hath my absence been
From thee, the pleasure of the fleeting year!
What freezings have I felt, what dark days seen!
What old December's bareness everywhere!
And yet this time removed was summer's time,
The teeming autumn big with rich increase,
Bearing the wanton burden of the prime,
Like widowed wombs after their lords' decease:
Yet this abundant issue seem'd to me
But hope of orphans, and unfathered fruit,
For summer and his pleasures wait on thee,
And thou away, the very birds are mute;
      Or if they sing, 'tis with so dull a cheer
      That leaves look pale, dreading the winter's near.

SONNET 98

From you have I been absent in the spring,
When proud-pied April (dressed in all his trim)
Hath put a spirit of youth in every thing,
That heavy Saturn laughed and leapt with him.
Yet nor the lays of birds, nor the sweet smell
Of different flowers in odour and in hue,
Could make me any summer's story tell,
Or from their proud lap pluck them while they grew:
Nor did I wonder at the lily's white,
Nor praise the deep vermilion in the rose;
They were but sweet, but figures of delight,
Drawn after you, you pattern of all those.
      Yet seemed it winter still, and, you away,
      As with your shadow I with these did play.

SONNET 99

The forward violet thus did I chide:
"Sweet thief, whence didst thou steal thy sweet that smells,
If not from my love's breath? The purple pride
Which on thy soft cheek for complexion dwells,
In my love's veins thou hast too grossly dyed."
The lily I condemned for thy hand,
And buds of marjoram had stol'n thy hair;
The roses fearfully on thorns did stand,
One blushing shame, another white despair;
A third, nor red nor white, had stol'n of both,
And to his robb'ry had annex'd thy breath;
But for his theft, in pride of all his growth,
A vengeful canker eat him up to death.
     More flowers I noted, yet I none could see
     But sweet or color it had stol'n from thee.

SONNET 100

Where art thou, Muse, that thou forget'st so long
To speak of that which gives thee all thy might?
Spend'st thou thy fury on some worthless song,
Dark'ning thy pow'r to lend base subjects light?
Return, forgetful Muse, and straight redeem
In gentle numbers time so idly spent;
Sing to the ear that doth thy lays esteem,
And gives thy pen both skill and argument.
Rise, resty Muse, my love's sweet face survey,
If Time have any wrinkle graven there;
If any, be a satire to decay,
And make Time's spoils despised every where.
     Give my love fame faster than Time wastes life;
     So thou prevent'st his scythe and crooked knife.

SONNET 101

O truant Muse, what shall be thy amends
For thy neglect of truth in beauty dyed?
Both truth and beauty on my love depends;
So dost thou too, and therein dignified.
Make answer, Muse; wilt thou not haply say,
"Truth needs no colour with his colour fixed,
Beauty no pencil, beauty's truth to lay;
But best is best, if never intermixed"?
Because he needs no praise, wilt thou be dumb?
Excuse not silence so, for't lies in thee
To make him much outlive a gilded tomb,
And to be praised of ages yet to be.
      Then do thy office, Muse; I teach thee how
      To make him seem long hence as he shows now.

SONNET 102

My love is strengthened though more weak in seeming;
I love not less, though less the show appear:
That love is merchandised whose rich esteeming
The owner's tongue doth publish every where.
Our love was new, and then but in the spring,
When I was wont to greet it with my lays,
As Philomel in summer's front doth sing,
And stops her pipe in growth of riper days:
Not that the summer is less pleasant now
Than when her mournful hymns did hush the night,
But that wild music burdens every bough,
And sweets grown common lose their dear delight.
      Therefore like her, I sometime hold
        my tongue,
      Because I would not dull you with my song.

SONNET 103

Alack, what poverty my Muse brings forth,
That, having such a scope to show her pride,
The argument all bare is of more worth
Than when it hath my added praise beside.
O blame me not if I no more can write!
Look in your glass, and there appears a face
That overgoes my blunt invention quite,
Dulling my lines, and doing me disgrace.
Were it not sinful then, striving to mend,
To mar the subject that before was well?
For to no other pass my verses tend
Than of your graces and your gifts to tell;
    And more, much more than in my verse can sit,
    Your own glass shows you, when you look in it.

SONNET 104

To me, fair friend, you never can be old,
For as you were when first your eye I eyed,
Such seems your beauty still. Three winters cold
Have from the forests shook three summers' pride;
Three beauteous springs to yellow autumn turned
In process of the seasons have I seen;
Three April perfumes in three hot Junes burned,
Since first I saw you fresh, which yet are green.
Ah yet doth beauty, like a dial hand,
Steal from his figure, and no pace perceived;
So your sweet hue, which methinks still doth stand,
Hath motion, and mine eye may be deceived;
    For fear of which, hear this thou age unbred:
    Ere you were born was beauty's summer dead.

SONNET 105

Let not my love be called idolatry,
Nor my beloved as an idol show,
Since all alike my songs and praises be
To one, of one, still such, and ever so.
Kind is my love today, tomorrow kind,
Still constant in a wondrous excellence;
Therefore my verse, to constancy confined,
One thing expressing, leaves out difference.
"Fair, kind, and true" is all my argument,
"Fair, kind, and true" varying to other words,
And in this change is my invention spent,
Three themes in one, which wondrous scope affords.
        Fair, kind, and true have often lived alone,
        Which three till now never kept seat in one.

SONNET 106

When in the chronicle of wasted time
I see descriptions of the fairest wights,
And beauty making beautiful old rhyme
In praise of ladies dead and lovely knights;
Then in the blazon of sweet beauty's best,
Of hand, of foot, of lip, of eye, of brow,
I see their antique pen would have expressed
Even such a beauty as you master now.
So all their praises are but prophecies
Of this our time, all you prefiguring,
And for they looked but with divining eyes,
They had not skill enough your worth to sing:
        For we, which now behold these present days,
        Have eyes to wonder, but lack tongues to praise.

SONNET 107

Not mine own fears, nor the prophetic soul
Of the wide world, dreaming on things to come,
Can yet the lease of my true love control,
Supposed as forfeit to a confined doom.
The mortal moon hath her eclipse endured,
And the sad augurs mock their own presage,
Incertainties now crown themselves assured,
And peace proclaims olives of endless age.
Now with the drops of this most balmy time
My love looks fresh, and Death to me subscribes,
Since spite of him I'll live in this poor rhyme,
While he insults o'er dull and speechless tribes.
      And thou in this shalt find thy monument,
      When tyrants' crests and tombs of brass are spent.

SONNET 108

What's in the brain that ink may character,
Which hath not figured to thee my true spirit?
What's new to speak, what now to register,
That may express my love, or thy dear merit?
Nothing, sweet boy; but yet, like prayers divine,
I must each day say o'er the very same,
Counting no old thing old, thou mine, I thine,
Even as when first I hallowed thy fair name.
So that eternal love in love's fresh case
Weighs not the dust and injury of age,
Nor gives to necessary wrinkles place,
But makes antiquity for aye his page,
      Finding the first conceit of love there bred,
      Where time and outward form would show it dead.

SONNET 109

O never say that I was false of heart,
Though absence seemed my flame to qualify;
As easy might I from my self depart
As from my soul, which in thy breast doth lie:
That is my home of love; if I have ranged,
Like him that travels I return again,
Just to the time, not with the time exchanged,
So that myself bring water for my stain.
Never believe, though in my nature reigned
All frailties that besiege all kinds of blood,
That it could so preposterously be stained
To leave for nothing all thy sum of good:
    For nothing this wide universe I call,
    Save thou, my rose; in it thou art my all.

SONNET 110

Alas 'tis true, I have gone here and there,
And made myself a motley to the view,
Gored mine own thoughts, sold cheap what is most dear,
Made old offences of affections new.
Most true it is that I have looked on truth
Askance and strangely; but, by all above,
These blenches gave my heart another youth,
And worse essays proved thee my best of love.
Now all is done, have what shall have no end:
Mine appetite I never more will grind
On newer proof, to try an older friend,
A god in love, to whom I am confined.
    Then give me welcome, next my heaven the best,
    Even to thy pure and most most loving breast.

SONNET 111

O for my sake do you with Fortune chide,
The guilty goddess of my harmful deeds,
That did not better for my life provide
Than public means which public manners breeds.
Thence comes it that my name receives a brand,
And almost thence my nature is subdued
To what it works in, like the dyer's hand.
Pity me then, and wish I were renewed,
Whilst like a willing patient I will drink
Potions of eisel 'gainst my strong infection;
No bitterness that I will bitter think,
Nor double penance to correct correction.
  Pity me then, dear friend, and I assure ye,
  Even that your pity is enough to cure me.

SONNET 112

Your love and pity doth th'impression fill
Which vulgar scandal stamped upon my brow,
For what care I who calls me well or ill,
So you o'er-green my bad, my good allow?
You are my all the world, and I must strive
To know my shames and praises from your tongue;
None else to me, nor I to none alive,
That my steeled sense or changes right or wrong.
In so profound abysm I throw all care
Of others' voices, that my adder's sense
To critic and to flatterer stopped are.
Mark how with my neglect I do dispense:
  You are so strongly in my purpose bred
  That all the world besides methinks th'are dead.

SONNET 113

Since I left you, mine eye is in my mind;
And that which governs me to go about
Doth part his function, and is partly blind,
Seems seeing, but effectually is out;
For it no form delivers to the heart
Of bird, of flow'r, or shape which it doth latch;
Of his quick objects hath the mind no part;
Nor his own vision holds what it doth catch:
For if it see the rud'st or gentlest sight,
The most sweet-favoured or deformed'st creature,
The mountain, or the sea, the day, or night,
The crow, or dove, it shapes them to your feature.
     Incapable of more, replete with you,
     My most true mind thus maketh mine eye untrue.

SONNET 114

Or whether doth my mind, being crowned with you,
Drink up the monarch's plague, this flattery?
Or whether shall I say mine eye saith true,
And that your love taught it this alchemy?
To make of monsters, and things indigest,
Such cherubins as your sweet self resemble,
Creating every bad a perfect best
As fast as objects to his beams assemble?
O 'tis the first, 'tis flatt'ry in my seeing,
And my great mind most kingly drinks it up;
Mine eye well knows what with his gust is 'greeing,
And to his palate doth prepare the cup.
     If it be poisoned, 'tis the lesser sin
     That mine eye loves it and doth first begin.

SONNET 115

Those lines that I before have writ do lie,
Even those that said I could not love you dearer;
Yet then my judgement knew no reason why
My most full flame should afterwards burn clearer.
But reckoning Time, whose millioned accidents
Creep in 'twixt vows, and change decrees of kings,
Tan sacred beauty, blunt the sharp'st intents,
Divert strong minds to th'course of alt'ring things—
Alas, why fearing of Time's tyranny,
Might I not then say "Now I love you best,"
When I was certain o'er incertainty,
Crowning the present, doubting of the rest?
  Love is a babe, then might I not say so,
  To give full growth to that which still doth grow.

SONNET 116

Let me not to the marriage of true minds
Admit impediments; love is not love
Which alters when it alteration finds,
Or bends with the remover to remove.
O no, it is an ever-fixed mark
That looks on tempests and is never shaken;
It is the star to every wand'ring bark,
Whose worth's unknown, although his height be taken.
Love's not Time's fool, though rosy lips and cheeks
Within his bending sickle's compass come;
Love alters not with his brief hours and weeks,
But bears it out even to the edge of doom.
  If this be error and upon me proved,
  I never writ, nor no man ever loved.

SONNET 117

Accuse me thus, that I have scanted all
Wherein I should your great deserts repay,
Forgot upon your dearest love to call,
Whereto all bonds do tie me day by day;
That I have frequent been with unknown minds,
And given to time your own dear-purchased right;
That I have hoisted sail to all the winds
Which should transport me farthest from your sight.
Book both my wilfulness and errors down,
And on just proof surmise accumulate;
Bring me within the level of your frown,
But shoot not at me in your wakened hate:
  Since my appeal says I did strive to prove
  The constancy and virtue of your love.

SONNET 118

Like as to make our appetites more keen
With eager compounds we our palate urge,
As, to prevent our maladies unseen,
We sicken to shun sickness when we purge:
Even so, being full of your ne'er-cloying sweetness,
To bitter sauces did I frame my feeding,
And, sick of welfare, found a kind of meetness
To be diseased ere that there was true needing.
Thus policy in love, t'anticipate
The ills that were not, grew to faults assured,
And brought to medicine a healthful state
Which, rank of goodness, would by ill be cured.
  But thence I learn, and find the lesson true,
  Drugs poison him that so fell sick of you.

SONNET 119

What potions have I drunk of Siren tears
Distilled from limbecks foul as hell within,
Applying fears to hopes, and hopes to fears,
Still losing when I saw myself to win!
What wretched errors hath my heart committed,
Whilst it hath thought itself so blessed never!
How have mine eyes out of their spheres been fitted
In the distraction of this madding fever!
O benefit of ill: now I find true
That better is by evil still made better,
And ruined love when it is built anew
Grows fairer than at first, more strong, far greater.
　　　So I return rebuked to my content,
　　　And gain by ills thrice more than I have spent.

SONNET 120

That you were once unkind befriends me now,
And for that sorrow which I then did feel
Needs must I under my transgression bow,
Unless my nerves were brass or hammered steel.
For if you were by my unkindness shaken
As I by yours, y'have passed a hell of time,
And I, a tyrant, have no leisure taken
To weigh how once I suffered in your crime.
O that our night of woe might have rememb'red
My deepest sense, how hard true sorrow hits,
And soon to you, as you to me then tend'red
The humble salve which wounded bosom fits!
　　　But that your trespass now becomes a fee;
　　　Mine ransoms yours, and yours must ransom me.

SONNET 121

'Tis better to be vile than vile esteemed,
When not to be receives reproach of being,
And the just pleasure lost, which is so deemed
Not by our feeling but by others' seeing.
For why should others' false adulterate eyes
Give salutation to my sportive blood?
Or on my frailties why are frailer spies,
Which in their wills count bad what I think good?
No, I am that I am, and they that level
At my abuses reckon up their own;
I may be straight though they themselves be bevel;
By their rank thoughts my deeds must not be shown,
      Unless this general evil they maintain:
      All men are bad, and in their badness reign.

SONNET 122

Thy gift, thy tables, are within my brain
Full charactered with lasting memory,
Which shall above that idle rank remain
Beyond all date, even to eternity;
Or, at the least, so long as brain and heart
Have faculty by nature to subsist;
Till each to razed oblivion yield his part
Of thee, thy record never can be missed.
That poor retention could not so much hold,
Nor need I tallies thy dear love to score;
Therefore to give them from me was I bold,
To trust those tables that receive thee more:
      To keep an adjunct to remember thee
      Were to import forgetfulness in me.

SONNET 123

No! Time, thou shalt not boast that I do change:
Thy pyramids built up with newer might
To me are nothing novel, nothing strange;
They are but dressings of a former sight.
Our dates are brief, and therefore we admire
What thou dost foist upon us that is old,
And rather make them born to our desire
Than think that we before have heard them told.
Thy registers and thee I both defy,
Not wond'ring at the present, nor the past,
For thy records, and what we see, doth lie,
Made more or less by thy continual haste.
     This I do vow and this shall ever be:
     I will be true despite thy scythe and thee.

SONNET 124

If my dear love were but the child of state,
It might for Fortune's bastard be unfathered,
As subject to Time's love, or to Time's hate,
Weeds among weeds, or flowers with flowers gathered.
No, it was builded far from accident;
It suffers not in smiling pomp, nor falls
Under the blow of thralled discontent,
Whereto th'inviting time our fashion calls.
It fears not Policy, that heretic,
Which works on leases of short-numb'red hours,
But all alone stands hugely politic,
That it nor grows with heat, nor drowns with show'rs.
     To this I witness call the fools of Time,
     Which die for goodness, who have lived for crime.

SONNET 125

Were't aught to me I bore the canopy,
With my extern the outward honouring,
Or laid great bases for eternity,
Which proves more short than waste or ruining?
Have I not seen dwellers on form and favour
Lose all, and more, by paying too much rent,
For compound sweet forgoing simple savour,
Pitiful thrivers, in their gazing spent?
No, let me be obsequious in thy heart,
And take thou my oblation, poor but free,
Which is not mixed with seconds, knows no art
But mutual render, only me for thee.
      Hence, thou suborned informer! A true soul
      When most impeached stands least in thy control.

SONNET 126

O thou my lovely boy, who in thy power
Dost hold Time's fickle glass, his sickle hour;
Who hast by waning grown, and therein show'st
Thy lovers withering, as thy sweet self grow'st;
If Nature (sovereign mistress over wrack),
As thou goest onwards still will pluck thee back,
She keeps thee to this purpose, that her skill
May Time disgrace, and wretched minutes kill.
Yet fear her, O thou minion of her pleasure,
She may detain, but not still keep, her treasure!
Her audit (though delayed) answered must be,
And her quietus is to render thee.

SONNET 127

In the old age black was not counted fair,
Or if it were it bore not beauty's name;
But now is black beauty's successive heir,
And beauty slandered with a bastard shame:
For since each hand hath put on Nature's power,
Fairing the foul with art's false borrowed face,
Sweet beauty hath no name, no holy bower,
But is profaned, if not lives in disgrace.
Therefore my mistress' eyes are raven black,
Her brows so suited, and they mourners seem
At such who not born fair no beauty lack,
Sland'ring creation with a false esteem:
      Yet so they mourn, becoming of their woe,
      That every tongue says beauty should look so.

SONNET 128

How oft when thou, my music, music play'st
Upon that blessed wood whose motion sounds
With thy sweet fingers when thou gently sway'st
The wiry concord that mine ear confounds,
Do I envy those jacks that nimble leap
To kiss the tender inward of thy hand,
Whilst my poor lips, which should that harvest reap,
At the wood's boldness by thee blushing stand.
To be so tickled they would change their state
And situation with those dancing chips
O'er whom thy fingers walk with gentle gait,
Making dead wood more blest than living lips.
      Since saucy jacks so happy are in this,
      Give them thy fingers, me thy lips to kiss.

SONNET 129

Th'expense of spirit in a waste of shame
Is lust in action, and till action, lust
Is perjured, murd'rous, bloody, full of blame,
Savage, extreme, rude, cruel, not to trust;
Enjoyed no sooner but despised straight,
Past reason hunted, and no sooner had,
Past reason hated as a swallowed bait
On purpose laid to make the taker mad:
Mad in pursuit and in possession so,
Had, having, and in quest to have, extreme;
A bliss in proof, and proved, a very woe,
Before, a joy proposed, behind, a dream.
      All this the world well knows yet none knows well
      To shun the heaven that leads men to this hell.

SONNET 130

My mistress' eyes are nothing like the sun,
Coral is far more red than her lips' red;
If snow be white, why then her breasts are dun;
If hairs be wires, black wires grow on her head.
I have seen roses damasked, red and white,
But no such roses see I in her cheeks,
And in some perfumes is there more delight
Than in the breath that from my mistress reeks.
I love to hear her speak, yet well I know
That music hath a far more pleasing sound;
I grant I never saw a goddess go:
My mistress when she walks treads on the ground.
      And yet by heaven I think my love as rare
      As any she belied with false compare.

SONNET 131

Thou art as tyrannous, so as thou art,
As those whose beauties proudly make them cruel;
For well thou know'st to my dear doting heart
Thou art the fairest and most precious jewel.
Yet in good faith some say that thee behold,
Thy face hath not the power to make love groan;
To say they err, I dare not be so bold,
Although I swear it to myself alone.
And to be sure that is not false I swear,
A thousand groans but thinking on thy face
One on another's neck do witness bear
Thy black is fairest in my judgement's place.
      In nothing art thou black save in thy deeds,
      And thence this slander as I think proceeds.

SONNET 132

Thine eyes I love, and they, as pitying me,
Knowing thy heart torment me with disdain,
Have put on black, and loving mourners be,
Looking with pretty ruth upon my pain.
And truly not the morning sun of heaven
Better becomes the grey cheeks of the east,
Nor that full star that ushers in the even
Doth half that glory to the sober west
As those two mourning eyes become thy face.
O let it then as well beseem thy heart
To mourn for me, since mourning doth thee grace,
And suit thy pity like in every part.
      Then will I swear beauty herself is black,
      And all they foul that thy complexion lack.

SONNET 133

Beshrew that heart that makes my heart to groan
For that deep wound it gives my friend and me.
Is't not enough to torture me alone,
But slave to slavery my sweet'st friend must be?
Me from myself thy cruel eye hath taken,
And my next self thou harder hast engrossed;
Of him, myself, and thee I am forsaken,
A torment thrice threefold thus to be crossed.
Prison my heart in thy steel bosom's ward,
But then my friend's heart let my poor heart bail;
Whoe'er keeps me, let my heart be his guard,
Thou canst not then use rigour in my jail.
     And yet thou wilt, for I, being pent in thee,
     Perforce am thine, and all that is in me.

SONNET 134

So now I have confessed that he is thine,
And I myself am mortgaged to thy will,
Myself I'll forfeit, so that other mine
Thou wilt restore to be my comfort still.
But thou wilt not, nor he will not be free,
For thou art covetous, and he is kind;
He learned but surety-like to write for me
Under that bond that him as fast doth bind.
The statute of thy beauty thou wilt take,
Thou usurer that put'st forth all to use,
And sue a friend came debtor for my sake,
So him I lose through my unkind abuse.
     Him have I lost, thou hast both him and me;
     He pays the whole, and yet I am not free.

SONNET 135

Whoever hath her wish, thou hast thy Will,
And Will to boot, and Will in overplus;
More than enough am I that vex thee still,
To thy sweet will making addition thus.
Wilt thou, whose will is large and spacious,
Not once vouchsafe to hide my will in thine?
Shall will in others seem right gracious,
And in my will no fair acceptance shine?
The sea, all water, yet receives rain still,
And in abundance addeth to his store;
So thou being rich in Will add to thy Will
One will of mine to make thy large Will more.
      Let no unkind, no fair beseechers kill;
      Think all but one, and me in that one Will.

SONNET 136

If thy soul check thee that I come so near,
Swear to thy blind soul that I was thy Will,
And will, thy soul knows, is admitted there;
Thus far for love, my love-suit, sweet, fulfil.
Will will fulfil the treasure of thy love,
Ay, fill it full with wills, and my will one.
In things of great receipt with ease we prove
Among a number one is reckoned none:
Then in the number let me pass untold,
Though in thy store's account I one must be;
For nothing hold me, so it please thee hold
That nothing me, a something sweet to thee.
      Make but my name thy love, and love that still,
      And then thou lov'st me for my name is Will.

SONNET 137

Thou blind fool, Love, what dost thou to mine eyes,
That they behold and see not what they see?
They know what beauty is, see where it lies,
Yet what the best is take the worst to be.
If eyes, corrupt by over-partial looks,
Be anchored in the bay where all men ride,
Why of eyes' falsehood hast thou forged hooks,
Whereto the judgement of my heart is tied?
Why should my heart think that a several plot,
Which my heart knows the wide world's common place?
Or mine eyes seeing this, say this is not,
To put fair truth upon so foul a face?
      In things right true my heart and eyes have erred,
      And to this false plague are they now transferred.

SONNET 138

When my love swears that she is made of truth,
I do believe her though I know she lies,
That she might think me some untutored youth,
Unlearned in the world's false subtleties.
Thus vainly thinking that she thinks me young,
Although she knows my days are past the best,
Simply I credit her false-speaking tongue:
On both sides thus is simple truth suppressed.
But wherefore says she not she is unjust?
And wherefore say not I that I am old?
O love's best habit is in seeming trust,
And age in love loves not to have years told.
      Therefore I lie with her, and she with me,
      And in our faults by lies we flattered be.

SONNET 139

O call not me to justify the wrong
That thy unkindness lays upon my heart;
Wound me not with thine eye but with thy tongue,
Use power with power, and slay me not by art.
Tell me thou lov'st elsewhere; but in my sight,
Dear heart, forbear to glance thine eye aside
What need'st thou wound with cunning when thy might
Is more than my o'erpressed defence can bide?
Let me excuse thee: "Ah, my love well knows
Her pretty looks have been mine enemies,
And therefore from my face she turns my foes,
That they elsewhere might dart their injuries."
　　　　Yet do not so, but since I am near slain,
　　　　Kill me outright with looks, and rid my pain.

SONNET 140

Be wise as thou art cruel, do not press
My tongue-tied patience with too much disdain,
Lest sorrow lend me words, and words express
The manner of my pity-wanting pain.
If I might teach thee wit, better it were,
Though not to love, yet, love, to tell me so—
As testy sick men, when their deaths be near,
No news but health from their physicians know.
For if I should despair I should grow mad,
And in my madness might speak ill of thee;
Now this ill-wresting world is grown so bad,
Mad slanderers by mad ears believed be.
　　　　That I may not be so, nor thou belied,
　　　　Bear thine eyes straight, though thy proud heart go wide.

SONNET 141

In faith, I do not love thee with mine eyes,
For they in thee a thousand errors note,
But 'tis my heart that loves what they despise,
Who in despite of view is pleased to dote.
Nor are mine ears with thy tongue's tune delighted,
Nor tender feeling to base touches prone,
Nor taste, nor smell, desire to be invited
To any sensual feast with thee alone;
But my five wits nor my five senses can
Dissuade one foolish heart from serving thee,
Who leaves unswayed the likeness of a man,
Thy proud heart's slave and vassal wretch to be.
  Only my plague thus far I count my gain,
  That she that makes me sin awards me pain.

SONNET 142

Love is my sin, and thy dear virtue hate,
Hate of my sin, grounded on sinful loving.
O but with mine compare thou thine own state,
And thou shalt find it merits not reproving,
Or if it do, not from those lips of thine,
That have profaned their scarlet ornaments,
And sealed false bonds of love as oft as mine,
Robbed others' beds' revenues of their rents.
Be it lawful I love thee as thou lov'st those
Whom thine eyes woo as mine importune thee.
Root pity in thy heart, that when it grows,
Thy pity may deserve to pitied be.
  If thou dost seek to have what thou dost hide,
  By self-example mayst thou be denied.

SONNET 143

Lo, as a careful housewife runs to catch
One of her feathered creatures broke away,
Sets down her babe and makes a swift dispatch
In pursuit of the thing she would have stay,
Whilst her neglected child holds her in chase,
Cries to catch her whose busy care is bent
To follow that which flies before her face,
Not prizing her poor infant's discontent:
So runn'st thou after that which flies from thee,
Whilst I, thy babe, chase thee afar behind;
But if thou catch thy hope, turn back to me
And play the mother's part, kiss me, be kind.
      So will I pray that thou mayst have thy Will,
      If thou turn back and my loud crying still.

SONNET 144

Two loves I have, of comfort and despair,
Which like two spirits do suggest me still:
The better angel is a man right fair;
The worser spirit a woman coloured ill.
To win me soon to hell my female evil
Tempteth my better angel from my side,
And would corrupt my saint to be a devil,
Wooing his purity with her foul pride.
And whether that my angel be turned fiend
Suspect I may, yet not directly tell,
But being both from me, both to each friend,
I guess one angel in another's hell.
      Yet this shall I ne'er know, but live in doubt,
      Till my bad angel fire my good one out.

SONNET 145

Those lips that Love's own hand did make
Breathed forth the sound that said "I hate"
To me that languished for her sake:
But when she saw my woeful state,
Straight in her heart did mercy come,
Chiding that tongue that ever sweet
Was used in giving gentle doom,
And taught it thus anew to greet:
"I hate" she altered with an end
That followed it as gentle day
Doth follow night, who like a fiend
From heaven to hell is flown away.
      "I hate" from hate away she threw,
      And saved my life, saying "not you."

SONNET 146

Poor soul, the center of my sinful earth,
Feeding these rebel pow'rs that thee array,
Why dost thou pine within and suffer dearth,
Painting thy outward walls so costly gay?
Why so large cost, having so short a lease,
Dost thou upon thy fading mansion spend?
Shall worms, inheritors of this excess,
Eat up thy charge? Is this thy body's end?
Then, soul, live thou upon thy servant's loss,
And let that pine to aggravate thy store;
Buy terms divine in selling hours of dross;
Within be fed, without be rich no more:
      So shalt thou feed on death, that feeds on men,
      And death once dead, there's no more dying then.

SONNET 147

My love is as a fever longing still
For that which longer nurseth the disease,
Feeding on that which doth preserve the ill,
Th'uncertain sickly appetite to please.
My reason, the physician to my love,
Angry that his prescriptions are not kept,
Hath left me, and I desperate, now approve
Desire is death, which physic did except.
Past cure I am, now reason is past care,
And frantic mad with evermore unrest;
My thoughts and my discourse as madmen's are,
At random from the truth vainly expressed:
>   For I have sworn thee fair, and thought thee bright,
>   Who art as black as hell, as dark as night.

SONNET 148

O me! what eyes hath love put in my head,
Which have no correspondence with true sight?
Or if they have, where is my judgement fled,
That censures falsely what they see aright?
If that be fair whereon my false eyes dote,
What means the world to say it is not so?
If it be not, then love doth well denote
Love's eye is not so true as all men's: no,
How can it? O how can love's eye be true,
That is so vexed with watching and with tears?
No marvel then though I mistake my view:
The sun itself sees not till heaven clears.
>   O cunning love, with tears thou keep'st me blind,
>   Lest eyes well seeing thy foul faults should find.

SONNET 149

Canst thou, O cruel, say I love thee not,
When I against myself with thee partake?
Do I not think on thee when I forgot
Am of myself, all tyrant for thy sake?
Who hateth thee that I do call my friend?
On whom frown'st thou that I do fawn upon?
Nay, if thou lour'st on me, do I not spend
Revenge upon myself with present moan?
What merit do I in myself respect
That is so proud thy service to despise,
When all my best doth worship thy defect,
Commanded by the motion of thine eyes?
      But, love, hate on, for now I know thy mind:
      Those that can see thou lov'st, and I am blind.

SONNET 150

O from what pow'r hast thou this pow'rful might,
With insufficiency my heart to sway,
To make me give the lie to my true sight,
And swear that brightness doth not grace the day?
Whence hast thou this becoming of things ill,
That in the very refuse of thy deeds
There is such strength and warrantise of skill
That in my mind thy worst all best exceeds?
Who taught thee how to make me love thee more,
The more I hear and see just cause of hate?
O, though I love what others do abhor,
With others thou shouldst not abhor my state:
      If thy unworthiness raised love in me,
      More worthy I to be beloved of thee.

SONNET 151

Love is too young to know what conscience is,
Yet who knows not conscience is born of love?
Then, gentle cheater, urge not my amiss,
Lest guilty of my faults thy sweet self prove.
For thou betraying me, I do betray
My nobler part to my gross body's treason;
My soul doth tell my body that he may
Triumph in love; flesh stays no farther reason,
But rising at thy name doth point out thee
As his triumphant prize; proud of this pride,
He is contented thy poor drudge to be,
To stand in thy affairs, fall by thy side.
        No want of conscience hold it that I call
        Her "love" for whose dear love I rise and fall.

SONNET 152

In loving thee thou know'st I am forsworn,
But thou art twice forsworn to me love swearing:
In act thy bed-vow broke, and new faith torn
In vowing new hate after new love bearing.
But why of two oaths' breach do I accuse thee,
When I break twenty? I am perjured most,
For all my vows are oaths but to misuse thee,
And all my honest faith in thee is lost.
For I have sworn deep oaths of thy deep kindness,
Oaths of thy love, thy truth, thy constancy,
And to enlighten thee gave eyes to blindness,
Or made them swear against the thing they see:
        For I have sworn thee fair: more perjured eye,
        To swear against the truth so foul a lie.

SONNET 153

Cupid laid by his brand and fell asleep:
A maid of Dian's this advantage found,
And his love-kindling fire did quickly steep
In a cold valley-fountain of that ground,
Which borrowed from this holy fire of Love
A dateless lively heat, still to endure,
And grew a seething bath, which yet men prove
Against strange maladies a sovereign cure.
But at my mistress' eye Love's brand new fired,
The boy for trial needs would touch my breast:
I, sick withal, the help of bath desired,
And thither hied, a sad distempered guest;
     But found no cure: the bath for my help lies
     Where Cupid got new fire: my mistress' eyes.

SONNET 154

The little Love-god lying once asleep
Laid by his side his heart-inflaming brand,
Whilst many nymphs that vowed chaste life to keep,
Came tripping by; but in her maiden hand
The fairest votary took up that fire
Which many legions of true hearts had warmed,
And so the general of hot desire
Was sleeping by a virgin hand disarmed.
This brand she quenched in a cool well by,
Which from Love's fire took heat perpetual,
Growing a bath and healthful remedy
For men diseased; but I, my mistress' thrall,
     Came there for cure, and this by that I prove:
     Love's fire heats water, water cools not love.

Bibliography

For a helpful guide to the scholarship and criticism of many commentaries, James Schiffer's introduction to *Shakespeare's Sonnets* (New York: Garland Publishing, 1998) is a very useful point of departure.

A brief select bibliography follows:

Auden, W. H. Introduction. *The Sonnets*, ed., William Burt. New York: New American Library (Signet), 1964.

Barber, C. L. "An Essay on Shakespeare's Sonnets," *The Sonnets of Shakespeare*. New York: Dell, 1960.

Bermann, Sandra. *The Sonnet Over Time: A Study of the Sonnets of Petrarch, Shakespeare, and Baudelaire.* Chapel Hill: University of North Carolina Press, 1988.

Blackmur, Richard. "A Poetics for Infatuation." *Outsider at the Heart of Things.* Champaign: University of Illinois Press, 1989.

Bloom, Harold, ed. *Shakespeare's Sonnets: Modern Critical Interpretations.* New York: Chelsea House, 1987.

Booth, Stephen. *An Essay on Shakespeare's Sonnets.* New Haven: Yale University Press, 1969.

———. *Shakespeare's Sonnets.* New Haven: Yale University Press, 1977.

Burrow, Colin, ed. *William Shakespeare: The Complete Sonnets and Poems.* New York: Oxford University Press, 2002.

Colie, Rosalie L. *Shakespeare's Living Art.* Princeton: Princeton University Press, 1974.

de Grazia, Margreta. "Locating and Dislocating the 'I' of Shakespeare's Sonnets." *William Shakespeare: His World, His Work, His Influence*, ed. John F. Andrews. Vol. 2. New York: Scribner's, 1985.

Dubrow, Heather. *Captive Victors: Shakespeare's Narrative Poems and Sonnets.* Ithaca: Cornell University Press, 1987.

BIBLIOGRAPHY

————. *Echoes of Desire: English Petrarchism and Its Counterdiscourses*. Ithaca: Cornell University Press, 1995.

————. "'Uncertainties now crown themselves assur'd': The Politics of Plotting Shakespeare's Sonnets." *Shakespeare Quarterly* 47 (1996).

Duncan-Jones, Katherine. "Was the 1609 *Shake-Speares Sonnets* Really Unauthorized?" *Review of English Studies* 34 (1984).

Empson, William. *Some Versions of the Pastoral*. 1935. New York: New Directions, 1974.

Evans, G. Blakemore, ed. *The Sonnets*. Cambridge: Cambridge University Press, 1996.

Ferry, Anne. *All in War with Time: Love Poetry of Shakespeare, Donne, Jonson, Marvell*. Cambridge, Mass.: Harvard University Press, 1975.

Fineman, Joel. *Shakespeare's Perjured Eye: The Invention of Poetic Subjectivity in the Sonnets*. Berkeley: University of California Press, 1986.

Goldberg, Jonathan. *Sodometries: Renaissance Texts, Modern Sexuality*. Stanford: Stanford University Press, 1992.

Hubler, Edward. *The Sense of Shakespeare's Sonnets*. Princeton: Princeton University Press, 1962.

———— et al., *The Riddle of Shakespeare's Sonnets*. New York: Basic Books, 1962.

Kernan, Alvin. "Shakepeare's Sonnets and Patronage Art." *Shakespeare, the King's Playwright: Theater in the Stuart Court, 1603–1613*. New Haven: Yale University Press, 1995.

Kerrigan, John, ed. *The Sonnets and A Lover's Complaint*. Harmondsworth, U.K.: Penguin, 1986.

Knight, L. C. "Shakespeare's Sonnets." *Scrutiny* 3 (1934).

Leisham, J. B. *Themes and Variations in Shakespeare's Sonnets*. New York: Harper and Row, 1961.

Lever, J. W. *The Elizabethan Love Sonnet*. London: Methuen, 1956.

Marotti, Arthur. "'Love Is Not Love': Elizabethan Sonnet Sequences and the Social Order." *ELH: English Literary History* 47:2 (1982).

Melchiori, Giorgio. *Shakespeare's Dramatic Meditations: An Experiment in Criticism*. Oxford: Clarendon, 1976.

Nowottny, Winifred. "Formal Elements in Shakespeare's Sonnets I–VI." *Essays in Criticism* 2 (1952).

Pequiney, Joseph. *Such Is My Love: A Study of Shakespeare's Sonnets*. Chicago: University of Chicago Press, 1985.

Roche, Thomas. *Petrarch and the English Sonnet Sequences*. New York: AMS, 1989.

Rollins, Hyder Edward, ed. *A New Variorum Edition of Shakespeare: The Sonnets*. 2 vols. Philadelphia: Lippincott, 1944.

Schalkwyk, David. *Speech and Performance in Shakespeare's Sonnets and Plays*. Cambridge: Cambridge University Press, 2002.

BIBLIOGRAPHY

Schiffer, James, ed. *Shakespeare's Sonnets: Critical Essays.* New York: Garland Publishing, 1998.

Sedgwick, Eve K. *Between Men: English Literature and Male Homosexual Desire.* New York: Columbia University Press, 1985.

Smith, Bruce. *Homosexual Desire in Shakespeare's England: A Cultural Poetics.* Chicago: University of Chicago Press, 1991.

Stallybrass, Peter. "Editing as Cultural Formation: The Sexing of Shakespeare's Sonnets." *Modern Language Quarterly* 54 (1997).

Stirling, Brents. *Shakespeare Sonnet Order: Poems and Groups.* Berkeley: University of California Press, 1968.

Vendler, Helen. *The Art of Shakespeare's Sonnets.* Cambridge, Mass.: Harvard University Press, 1997.

Acknowledgments

The idea for this book emerged in the mid-1960s, and grew partly out of many conversations with a Harvard colleague, David Kalstone. At the time, I was also stimulated by the work of some of my tutorial students, including Heather Dubrow, who has written on the Sonnets in a highly illuminating way. Later, invaluable talks with the late Paul Alpers helped further my ideas. Several friends have been kind enough to read and comment upon parts of the manuscript, in particular Jean Strouse. Helen Vendler's invaluable commentary on the Sonnets has been a constant point of reference for me. Jonathan Galassi offered very helpful comments and encouraged me to continue the book. Finally, my wife, Angelica Zander Rudenstine, provided all the editorial help that any writer might hope to receive.

Printed in the USA
CPSIA information can be obtained
at www.ICGtesting.com
LVHW091141150724
785511LV00005B/466

9 780374 535735